THE JUDGE

Also by the author

In His Own Image

THE
JUDGE

JAMES F. SIMON

David McKay Company, Inc.

NEW YORK

Library of Congress Cataloging in Publication Data

Simon, James F
The judge.

1. Judges—United States. 2. Criminal justice,
Administration of—United States. I. Title.
KF8785.S5   347'.73   75-45347
ISBN 0-679-50552-0

For Lauren, David, and Marcia

Author's Note

This book focuses on a state criminal court judge in a city in the northeastern part of the United States. All names and, when necessary, descriptive details of people and cases have been changed to prevent identification. The judge's observations and experiences, reported over many months, have been presented in the condensed and dramatized form of a single, composite week in the judge's life. The real "Judge Barth" donated, literally, hundreds of hours of his time for my interviews without making a single demand on me. For his time, understanding, and patience, I am deeply grateful. But we both understand that this is my book, not his, and that I, alone, am responsible for the contents.

I
Monday

7:31 A.M.

Judge James Barth looks in the bathroom mirror and is not particularly pleased with what he sees. He is fifty-three years old and it shows. Each month, it seems to him, he adds a few more gray hairs at the temples. He rubs his second chin, the one that has emerged simultaneously with his spreading waistline. Helen is right. He's got to use the exercise cycle more often and stay away from that new Italian restaurant around the corner from the courthouse.

After he shaves, he returns to his bedroom, where Helen is still sleeping. Quietly, he puts on a pair of three-year-old gray flannel slacks, a fresh tee shirt, and black and red argyle socks, his substitute for bedroom slippers. With his fingers, he gives one quick rake through his thinning black hair and tiptoes out of the room. Deftly, he navigates past his exercise cycle in the hallway and arrives at the kitchen door where Helen's potted Schefflera stands guard.

Feeling more ambitious than usual, Barth washes the cups

(3)

and saucers in the sink. Helen will like that. He rewards himself for his good deed by plugging in the percolator for his first cup of black coffee.

At eight o'clock he flips on the radio for the hour's headlines. They aren't very different from last week's or last month's, which makes him wonder why he bothers to listen. The highlight of the broadcast is the weather report. Barth learns that this Monday will be a bright, sunlit spring day. He pays particular attention to the announcement of the pollen count. Somehow, Barth cares about the pollen count. If the count is low, he begins to feel good about the day. And today the count is below normal. Yes, he tells himself, it is going to be a good day.

John Harding's long black legs lie straight across the mattress, like stilts at rest. His hands are clasped together behind his head. Harding stares at the concrete ceiling of his cell. It is gray and depressing but his eyes do not seem to notice. They focus on a single crack, just above his head, that is distinguished from the rest of the cracks on the 8′ by 12′ ceiling only because it happens to be directly above Harding's head. Below Harding, on the lower bunk, is another body, loudly sleeping, and there are two more beds and two more bodies pushed against the opposite wall.

For two hours Harding has not looked at the other three men in the cell, or the latrine in the corner, or the bars, but only at that single crack in the ceiling. And for two hours Harding appears to have heard no sounds outside his own head, not the groans, the shrieks, the agonized mumbles of those in surrounding cells, nor the yells of the guards, the sputters and gurgles of the old radiators. Nothing.

"Harding," shouts a guard. "Harding."

Slowly, the lank body begins to move into a sitting position at the tip of the bunk, then drops to the floor. Harding slips his feet into black patent leather loafers, carefully tucks his white shirt into his brown corduroy pants, and stands impassively. The guard opens the door and prepares to lead Harding to another cell, this one adjacent to Courtroom 27, where he is on trial, charged with assault and armed robbery, before the Honorable James Barth, State Criminal Court Judge.

9:23 A.M.

Barth looks admiringly at the interior of the courthouse rotunda. Every other judge in the building gripes about the extravagant architecture, but not Barth. He loves the Ionic columns, even if they don't hold up anything. And he likes to trace history daily through the panoramic mural painted just above the columns. So what if it was a WPA project and some of the participants were better qualified to paint cellar doors than Sistine ceilings? And what if the foreshortened arms of the Egyptian pharaohs and the countenance of old Abe Lincoln are not quite believable? Still, Barth thinks there is something inspiring in the attempt, if not the execution. Besides, it gives him something to look at while he waits for the elevator to make its way up, glacierlike, from the basement.

As he paces in front of the elevator door, Barth's thoughts turn to John Harding. Judging from the police report, young Harding is in serious trouble. Karen Petersen told police that Harding slit her throat and then took $2,400 from an office safe. Since it all happened in the office where Harding worked with Miss Petersen, identification of the defendant by Petersen and her office assistant is probably going to impress the jury.

How will the jury react? That ought to be a primary consideration for Barbara Jennings, Harding's attorney. Forget about that blind lady with the scales. Forget about Perry Mason and Owen Marshall and the rest of the mythical heroes. The fact is that juries, not lofty principles or scriptwriters' rhetoric, decide cases. And like the rest of us, jurors are impressionable human beings. A jury of twelve law-abiding citizens is likely to squirm when it is told a story of assault and can look at a traumatized victim, with twenty-eight stitches to prove the agony.

Barbara Jennings should have pushed Harding to take a plea. With a little charm and shrewdness, she could have talked the DA into an attempted armed robbery plea. That would give Harding a lot less state time than he risks with a trial and conviction on charges of armed robbery and assault. In exchange, the DA could have saved himself trial time and eliminated the possibility of an acquittal. A solid bargain. But Harding wouldn't even consider a plea. Why?

Barth offers himself three quick explanations. First, John Harding simply does not understand how serious his situation is and, therefore, is incapable of making a rational decision to take a plea. Second, Harding understands his situation very well indeed but is a gambler; he likes his chances for acquittal before this jury. And finally, there's the possibility that Harding is innocent and he'll be damned if he'll cop a plea just to ease the burdens of the state's criminal justice system. Well, I'll probably never know why Harding has refused to take a plea, but I will know soon enough if his decision was a wise one.

"Good morning, Your Honor," barks a court officer as Barth steps off the elevator.

"Good morning," says Barth in his raspy, street-wise voice.

The court officer motions Barth to follow him, and the two walk down the corridor crowded with people and sounds and extravagant smells. Pimps in high-brimmed hats and alligator shoes smile benignly on the painted faces of their prostitutes. Mothers in brown cloth coats give last kisses to their bell-bottomed sons, who, on this sentencing day, may not come home again. Fast-talking lawyers counsel sleepy-eyed repeaters.

Friends laugh too loudly at each other's jokes. Babies cry and so do lovers.

The officer waits at the door leading to Barth's robing room while Barth inserts his key in the lock. Once the door is opened, the officer snaps to attention and bids Barth a good day. That daily ritual always makes Barth think of *The New Yorker* cartoon that he has pasted on his robing-room wall. One judge says to another: "This daily metamorphosis never fails to amaze me. At home, I'm an absolute idiot. But once I put on the black robes, by God, I'm it."

Barth reflects on the attention created by the power of his office. Court officers open doors for him, lawyers thank him for doing the job that allows him to earn more than $35,000 a year, defendants sometimes cry in gratitude, and strangers address him as "Your Honor." Those fringe benefits are nice but they are not the real reasons that Barth is fascinated with his role as a judge. One of those reasons has to do with the uses of power and authority. How do you make someone do what you think ought to be done in a civilized society, short of beating him over the head? You try to do it with legal rules and with Judge James Barth's authority to enforce those rules.

Barth walks through his robing room without a pause and enters the courtroom in his rumpled brown tweed suit. He has not worn a black robe in his courtroom for the last two years. Part of the reason is that he considers it a silly-looking costume. But his decision is based on more than stylistic preference. He has to get along with many different kinds of people in his job. In the current climate, he figures that the less he looks like "the establishment," the better off he is.

George Giles, Barth's court clerk, greets him with a warm, "Good morning, Judge." Giles is a hulking six-foot, four-inch ex-paratrooper with a weakness for Kawasaki motorcycles (he has two). Barth is still congratulating himself on his good fortune in finding Giles, a clerk whose temperament and work habits match his own. Like Barth, Giles attacks idle time compulsively. Neither Barth nor Giles minds asserting himself, even when the assertion may push him to the boundaries of his authority. Each wants a distinctive piece of whatever action happens to be going on in Courtroom 27. While Barth sorts out defendants' pasts and futures, George Giles deals with their names and statistics on the courtroom calendar. Giles never second guesses Barth's judgments, and Barth does not question Giles command of the calendar. Courthouse rumor has it that Giles and Barth have been together so long (three years) because nobody else in the building could possibly tolerate either of them.

Barth takes the two familiar steps to the bench and sits down heavily in his large leather chair. Directly above his head is the broadly lettered IN GOD WE TRUST. Courtroom 27 was designed in the nineteen thirties, when institutional architects favored church motifs. Like every other courtroom in the building, it is graced with high ceilings and long, wooden benches fastened to the floor. Beyond that, however, there is little to inspire. The windows that begin halfway up the north wall and reach to the ceiling are dirty and half hidden by broken venetian blinds. Light green paint, fresh two years ago, is now peeling from the walls. At least a dozen of the scuffed brown linoleum floor panels are cracked. But practically no one notices since three of the large fluorescent lights above them are out.

Only two people are sitting in the twelve rows of wooden benches in the public gallery. One is Mrs. Murphy, wearing her favorite gray shawl and blue dress and covertly munching Cracker Jacks from a box that she has freshly opened in honor of Judge Barth's Monday calendar. Like the other courthouse regulars, Mrs. Murphy does not squander her social security payments on such frivolous and expensive entertainment as movies; in court, the action is free and continuous. Barth likes to think that Mrs. Murphy picks his courtroom morning after morning because of her discriminating judicial tastes.

The other spectator is a black man who sits in the front pew, erect and anguished. His dark brown eyes dart nervously from the bench to the side door leading to the city jail and back again. He has made the morning tabloid newspaper into a tightly folded paper switch which he is thumping methodically across his right trouser leg. He must be a relative of John Harding's, Barth surmises.

Barth's two court officers, Sam Mitchell and Alfred Lorenzo, are chatting at the railing separating the public gallery from the trial area. Their identical blue uniforms do little to hide their contrasting appearances. Mitchell, a black who once was clocked at 9.4 seconds in the 100-yard dash, is lithe at the same 160 pounds he carried in track meets two decades ago. Alfred Lorenzo, whose skin is pale white, has added 30 pounds to his already considerable body since his wife died last year. Now he weighs 248 pounds, most of which has gravitated to his enormous gut, challenging daily the buttons and linings of his extra-large uniform.

Barth motions George Giles to the bench to tell him he wants John Harding; Harding's attorney, Barbara Jennings; Assistant District Attorney Bob Carlin; and the Harding jury in his courtroom in five minutes ready for trial. In the meantime, Barth places two books, both thick and punctuated with paperclips, directly in front of him. They are his indispensable reference books, the *State Penal Code* and the *State Code of Criminal Procedure*. To the side, Barth keeps a yellow handbook for judges, sent to him by Chief Administrative Judge John Talbert. The handbook informs Barth, among other things, as to why it is unethical for a judge to practice law, how he should define the crime of armed robbery in the first degree for a jury, and what are the official legal holidays. Just below Christmas

(9)

on the holiday list, Barth has added in longhand the dates of the Kentucky Derby, the Preakness, and the Belmont Stakes.

Barth also keeps a copy of the Old Testament for easy reference. It is not for spiritual guidance. During particularly long and boring jury selections, Barth turns to the back of the Bible where he has begun an elaborate annotation: bail jump escape—Proverbs 28:1 ("The wicked man fleeth, when no man pursueth: but the just, bold as a lion, shall be without dread"); knifing—Numbers 35:16 ("If any man strike with iron, and he die that was struck: he shall be guilty of murder, and he himself shall die"); murder—Exodus 2:12 ("And when he had looked about this way and that way, and saw no one there, he slew the Egyptian and hid him in the sand").

John Harding enters the courtroom, escorted to the defense table by Court Officer Sam Mitchell. When he sits down, his long legs brush against the bottom of the table. His attorney, Barbara Jennings, twenty-five, sits next to him, nervously scribbling notes on a pad of yellow legal paper. Her brown hair is swept back into a tight bun. She wears a well-tailored black and white checked pants suit and a dark red turtleneck sweater. Her even features, like her pants suit, are quietly attractive. She looks up briefly, smiles at Harding, then resumes her last-minute note-taking.

At the prosecutor's table across the aisle from Barbara Jennings, sits Bob Carlin, the twenty-eight-year-old assistant district attorney. Around the DA's office, Carlin is kidded about his modish dress. Today, he is in full flower. His double-breasted silver gray suit is perfectly cut to his modest five-foot eight-inch frame. His shirt collar is white but below it is an aggressive red paisley pattern. Carlin's sandy hair spills carefully over his coat collar. His oversized aviator glasses overwhelm his smooth, boyish features.

The twelve jurors take their places in the jury box, which is

(10)

separated from Bob Carlin's table by four feet and a wooden railing. The jurors come in all shapes, sizes, and colors. Among them are a bus driver, a hospital orderly, a social worker, and a retired vacuum cleaner salesman. There are three blacks, one Puerto Rican, and four women. The foreman, a bespectacled blond, teaches American history at a local high school.

"The People versus John Harding," intones George Giles. "Is the defense ready?"

"Yes," says Barbara Jennings.

"Are the People ready?" asks Giles.

"Yes," replies Bob Carlin.

"Mr. Carlin, call your first witness," Barth says.

"The People call Miss Karen Petersen," the DA replies.

Karen Petersen, thirty-three years old, walks to the witness stand with tense, quick steps. She has long, silky blond hair swept over her forehead, clear blue eyes, upturned nose and full, sensuous lips. Her brown wool suit does not advertise her shapely figure but does not hide it either. When she sits down and her skirt stops two inches above her knees, it is clear to all twelve jurors that Karen Petersen is a very attractive woman.

"The witness states her name as Karen Petersen. P as in Peter, E, T as in Thomas, E, R, S, E, N as in Nancy," shouts Court Officer Alfred Lorenzo, playing his fifteen-second bit part to the hilt.

Karen Petersen is terrified. Not nervous, but terrified. It shows in the anxious blinking of her eyes, in the pursing of her lips and in the handkerchief that she has knotted around her right hand.

"Please relax, Miss Petersen," Carlin says in a quiet, intentionally soothing voice.

But she can't. In giving basic background information, she speaks in short, brittle phrases. She testifies that she has been in the food service business for eleven years, exactly the time she has lived in the United States since leaving her native Sweden.

(11)

Her current position is that of food supervisor for bank employees at the cafeteria on the fourteenth floor of the Liberty National Bank Building, 1480 Broad Street.

As Carlin guides Karen Petersen slowly to the events that have led to her court appearance, the witness's body tightens. With a slight Swedish accent, she tells of her first meeting with John Harding, on June 11, 1973, the day she returned to work from a two-week vacation. Harding, who had been hired as a pot washer during her absence the week before, asked Miss Petersen for an advance of $20 on his week's salary. She gave him the $20 advance without argument. The next day, Harding again asked her for a $20 advance and, again, Karen Petersen approved it. As she tells her story, the witness takes furtive, pained glimpses of John Harding, who sits calmly at the defense table. On Friday, June 15, Miss Petersen testifies, John Harding collected his salary check but did not pay back the advances. John Harding did not show up for work the next week, she says, nor did he make any effort to repay the advances.

"The following Friday, John came into my office after the cafeteria had closed. It was about three P.M., and I was making out the food orders for the next day. My office girl, Mrs. Mendoza, was helping me. John asked to speak to me about the 'mistake' from the previous week. I told him that it was out of my hands, that I had told my supervisor what had happened. I also told John that he was lucky I had not called the police. John then asked if there was anything he could do to correct his mistake. I told him he could work here every Friday until he had repaid the money he had taken. John agreed to it and left."

There is no movement in the courtroom. The jurors, the judge, the clerk, the attorneys all listen intently to every word. Only John Harding seems relaxed, slumping slightly in his chair.

Karen Petersen tells her story compulsively now, so that

Carlin has no work at all except to say, "And then what happened?"

"Twenty minutes after John Harding left," Karen Petersen continues, "I was still sitting in my office. Suddenly, someone came up behind me, grabbed me by the neck, and lifted me out of my chair." The witness's neck jerks back, her eyes dart to the defendant's table. "Mrs. Mendoza screamed, 'John, what are you doing?' I turned my head and could see John Harding behind me."

"What happened next, Miss Petersen?" asks Carlin.

"John put a knife to my neck and asked, 'Where is the money?' I told Mrs. Mendoza to give John the money in my pocketbook. But he said he wanted the money in the safe. I told Mrs. Mendoza to open the safe. John then ordered me to lie down on the floor on my stomach. After Mrs. Mendoza opened the safe, she placed all of the cash receipts from the safe on my desk."

"And what was the amount of the cash in the safe that Mrs. Mendoza had put on your desk?" asks Carlin.

"Twenty-four hundred dollars," Miss Petersen replies.

"Are you certain of that amount?"

"Yes," she says. "Earlier that day I reviewed the cash receipts for the week."

"Go on, Miss Petersen."

"John ordered Mrs. Mendoza to lie down next to me. I looked up at John and pleaded with him not to do this terrible thing. Mrs. Mendoza also pleaded with him. But he kept saying, 'Shut up, Petersen; shut up, Mendoza.'"

"And then what happened?" asks Carlin.

"John tied my hands with strips of curtain that he had gotten from the office closet. I tried to get up and call for help. He hit me on the jaw." The witness flinches, as she tells of Harding striking her. "And then . . ." the witness hesitates momentarily. Then she blurts out:

"And then he asked me if I'd ever been fucked by a black

(13)

man." The words spill out as if the witness thinks that the faster she says them, the quicker the memory will be forgotten. Karen Petersen appears on the verge of tears. But she straightens up and finishes the thought in firm, even tones. "He said that he would do it if he had time." Karen Petersen looks straight at the jury as she tells of the defendant's threat.

"Please continue, Miss Petersen," says Carlin.

"The next thing I remember was that I felt a sensation at my throat," the witness says, putting her hands to her throat. "John said that he had cut my throat," she stammers now, "because I was being so mean."

Again, the witness seems to tell herself to settle down and continues the narrative in a controlled voice. "I saw John put the money in a briefcase. He asked me if I had ever heard of the Black Liberation Movement. He said the money would send black people to Russia. Then he wiped the desk and the doorknob with a handkerchief and left."

"What happened then?" asks Carlin.

"Mrs. Mendoza picked up the telephone and called the security office for help. A few minutes later a nurse and doctor arrived. I was taken to the hospital, where I received twenty-eight stitches for the cut across my throat."

"Miss Petersen," Carlin interrupts, "could you show the jury where you received the stitches?"

Karen Petersen slowly pushes back the high collar of her blouse and, with an agonized look at the jury, displays the scar. It is a thick, white, incongruously neat line that stretches from one side of her neck to the other.

Carlin pauses to let the jury ponder the scar and agony of the witness. "Miss Petersen, when did you speak to the police about the incident?"

"That same afternoon. They came to the hospital and I told them that John Harding had done this."

"Miss Petersen," Carlin continues, "how long was the defendant, John Harding, in your office the afternoon of the assault and robbery?"

"I would say about fifteen minutes," the witness replies.

"And during that fifteen minutes how much time would you say that you were actually looking at John Harding?"

"For about five minutes."

"Now, Miss Petersen, are you certain that the man who took the money from your office safe and slit your throat was John Harding?"

"Yes."

"And you are certain that it is the same John Harding who sits at the defense table?"

"Absolutely."

"I have no further questions, Your Honor," says Carlin.

During the walk to his chambers, Barth analyzes the Harding case: I think John Harding wanted to quit his job and was looking for an excuse to do it. So he went to Karen Petersen and demanded a $20 advance, not thinking he would get it. She frustrated him by giving it to him. He tried it again the next day and the same thing happened. He was still looking for a hostile reaction and didn't find it. So he quit without paying back the advances and, even then, Karen Petersen did nothing except to say he could pay the money back in weekly installments. Harding came back a second time that day out of sheer frustration. He wanted to force the issue. I don't think when he came back he had any idea of taking the money from the safe or assaulting Miss Petersen. He came back because he wanted some hostile reaction from her that would justify his quitting.

Mr. Harding's problem was that Karen Petersen had none of the hostility toward blacks of most white American females. She's a Swede and she just doesn't have that hang-up. And it infuriated him and led him to do what he did. I could be

(15)

wrong, but my theory makes a lot of sense to me. After lunch, maybe I can get Carlin and Barbara Jennings together on a plea that Harding will accept and help him out of this mess.

1:03 P.M.

"What's doing, Betsy?" asks Barth as he rushes by his secretary, Betsy Wilkinson.

"Everything's quiet, Judge."

"Good," he says as he pushes open his chambers door, ignoring his stenciled caveat: BEFORE ENTERING, THINK THREE TIMES—IS IT NECESSARY TO DISTURB HIM?

Barth has made his chambers his second home and has done it, he will tell you proudly, with considerably less money than he is entitled to in the state budget. That is more than can be said for many of his colleagues, particularly those who consider their appointments a social, as well as professional, step up in the world. They hire high-priced interior decorators who advise them to buy lush drapes, oriental rugs, and $200 potted plants. Having gone through their budgets in a morning, they are forced to take bank loans on the side to complete the job.

Not Barth. On his first trip to his office five years ago, Barth took one look at the solid, brown oak desk that his predecessor had left—it was not stylishly sleek—and decided he would keep it. It was a perfectly fine desk. Besides, Barth had a hunch that solid, brown oak desks would come back into style before his judicial term expired.

According to the state law, which Barth had scrutinized, the Public Works Department presented judges with many decorative opportunities that would not cost them a dime. Barth could and did have members of the department stain eight conference chairs to match his conference table, which he had moved over from his old law office. He also requested that the

Public Works Department fit the chairs with handsome red leather upholstery. In Barth's opinion, those small requests had given him one of the most attractive conference sets in the building. And he still had his state budgetary allotment.

Helen Barth had donated a large asparagus fern on the condition that her husband would give it hospitable quarters. Barth walked down to his favorite antique shop and promptly bought a brass barber's basin which, he decided, supported Helen's plant in grand style.

Instead of hanging the usual photographs and paintings of distinguished judges on the wall facing his shelves of law books, Barth displays Thomas Nast cartoons from the old *Harper's Weekly*, lampooning the likes of President Grant and Boss Tweed. Barth could not resist one final political touch. Long a collector of campaign buttons, Barth purchased a plain glass exhibition case and lined up buttons with the slogans and grins of more than a hundred politicians, from Al Smith to Richard Nixon.

The elaborate certificate of election to the court, hanging on the wall to the left of his desk, makes Barth smile. Like every other judge on his court, Barth was elected because of political clout, not merit. Most of his judicial colleagues had walked the traditional road to election, working in the local political wards until their time for the spoils arrived. To qualify, they had to be loyal, not intelligent or competent. Many of those in black robes today had begun less auspiciously, licking stamps, peddling campaign literature, staying in line with the regulars when their consciences told them to bolt.

Barth had followed another path: As an attorney, Barth's reputation for legal acumen in political elections had grown to the point where a candidate for local or state office hired him just to show he was serious. Barth, in turn, assured each client that he could run his campaign as he pleased and Jimmy Barth would take care of the legal fine points of the election laws. Barth knew how to word petitions, where to find the necessary signatures, when to scream fraud and how to demand a recount.

As a result, there was almost no politician on either side of the aisle in the state assembly who didn't owe Barth some small favor. If Barth's name was placed in nomination for a judgeship, therefore, nobody was going to squawk. Five years ago, one of the state's most powerful politicians, whom Barth had represented for many years, called to make the proposal. How would Barth like to be a state criminal court judge? If he was interested, Barth's client could guarantee his nomination and election. Barth pondered the offer, thinking out loud that the judicial robes might be too confining. "Look, Jimmy," the voice at the other end of the phone argued, "if you don't like it, you can quit and people will still call you 'Judge' for the rest of your life." Barth liked the logic and irreverence of the argument and accepted the offer.

On the conference table in his chambers Betsy has prepared what Barth thinks of unhappily as a "cat food" lunch: cold salmon out of a can, asparagus spears, tomatoes, and lettuce. Barth curses the bottle of diet Roquefort dressing. Even his secretary has to remind him of his weight problem. Next to the lunch, Barth's legal assistant, Melvin Rich, has placed a stack of probation department folders for defendants Barth must sentence this week.

Just as he sits down to lunch, the extension button on the office telephone lights up.

"A Mrs. Ethel Grace Warner would like to speak to you, Judge," Betsy says.

Ethel Grace Warner, Ethel Grace Warner. Barth tries to place the name. Oh, yes. Ethel Grace was one of Helen's college friends. I don't think we've seen her for ten years. Now I wonder what she wants to see me about. Whatever it is, it'll have to wait. I want to work on these folders now.

Barth presses the intercom. "Betsy, tell her to come back late this afternoon or tomorrow."

Almost instantly, the phone lights up again. "Judge, she says it can't wait. But she says she hopes it won't take very long."

"All right," Barth sighs. "Tell her to come on up." Now what does Ethel Warner have to tell me that's so urgent? He takes several bits of the salmon, and washes it down with gulps of water.

Five minutes later, Betsy knocks on the judge's door and ushers in a woman in her early fifties, arms outstretched. "Hi, Jimmy," Ethel Warner gushes, bussing Barth on the cheek.

Barth returns her greeting with a guarded smile. "It's good to see you, Ethel."

"You remember my husband, Marvin Warner?"

"Sure, how are you?" says Barth as he shakes hands with a small, diffident man who has suddenly appeared behind Ethel Warner.

"How's the family?" asks Ethel.

"Oh, they're just fine. You remember Bobby? Well, he's started law school this year. He's already begun to reverse my judicial decisions at the dinner table when he's home for weekends."

"Go on. You're as proud of him as you can be. And Helen, is she as beautiful and charming as ever?"

"Helen's fine," says Barth, almost curtly. He's still wondering what Ethel Warner wants. "Ethel, what can I do for you?"

At that moment, two people who have trailed into the office behind the Warners come forward.

"I'd like for you to meet Dorothy Livingston and Charles Moore. Dorothy and I have played bridge together for fifteen years. Charlie is an old high school chum of Marvin's. Last month, Marvin and I were planning a party and, of course, invited Dorothy. Marvin says to me, 'Ethel, do you mind if I invite an old friend who's in town on business?' I said, 'Of course not, Marvin.' The friend turned out to be Charlie. He met Dorothy at the party and you can probably guess the rest. They fell in love and now they want to get married. Can you do it, Jimmy?"

"Try to stop me," says Barth with feigned gruffness.

Charles Moore shakes Barth's hand vigorously. He is a stout, balding man who is trying, unsuccessfully, to hide his nervousness.

"Pleased to meet you, Mr. Moore," says Barth. Then Barth shakes hands with the bride, Dorothy Livingston, a once handsome woman whose tired face and slightly bowed body reflect the strain of the years.

"Betsy," Barth shouts, "get me a marriage form." When his secretary brings the certificate in, Barth goes to his desk and hastily fills in the blanks, asking the couple for information when he needs it. These details out of the way, Barth stands up and says, "Let's go." He directs the couple to stand in the corner between his framed political campaign buttons and a Thomas Nast lithograph of a venal Boss Tweed puppeteering with two politicians.

Barth suspects that this couple has been through it all before and may well go through it again. This time around there is no altar with flowers, no fresh young bridesmaids, no frocked minister to link them in holy wedlock. No, it is Jimmy Barth, a criminal court judge, who is delivering the vows in his rough, rasping accent.

Barth is certain that Dorothy Livingston and Charles Moore are more interested in the certificate than in anything he will say. He quickly opens a black book and begins to read. "We are gathered here today . . ." The couple looks straight ahead, smiles frozen. Barth completes the short service and pronounces Dorothy Livingston and Charles Moore man and wife.

Moore puts his hands on his new bride's cheeks, then kisses her on the lips. His eyes are open as are hers and their embrace is brief. There is pain reflected in the lines of their faces. But now there is also warmth and gentleness in their eyes, and hope that maybe, this time, it can work.

"Thanks so much," says Ethel Warner to Barth. "Give my regards to the family."

"I'll do that, Ethel," says Barth, smiling. "Good luck to all of you."

Barth closes the door and looks at the folders beside his half-eaten lunch. What's more important? he asks himself: Barth joining a couple in matrimony or Barth devoting yet another hour deciding whether a man should do ten years or twenty years in that miserable hellhole called the state penitentiary? No contest. He grabs an apple and hurries to the elevator, where he meets a colleague, Judge Walter Arnold. Arnold is a friendly gnome of a man in his early sixties. He is known among his colleagues as "the scholar," which, Barth figures, is not too difficult, given the competition.

"That's a nice suit," Arnold comments.

"I wish they had it in my size," Barth replies.

Arnold smiles admiringly and says to the elevator operator, "You can't top him, can you?" Turning to Barth, Arnold says, "You know, things were a little slow and I asked for more work. So Talbert gave me a real tough homicide case and it's about to get the better of me."

The elevator door opens and Arnold leaves quickly.

"I'll bet he wasn't in da army," the elevator operator says to Barth, "or he'd a learned, don't volunteer for nothin'."

2:16 P.M.

When Bob Carlin had first been asked to a conference in a judge's robing room, he had envisioned soft, velour curtains, Gilbert Stuart portraits and Chippendale chests. The robing room of Judge James Barth, and that of every other state criminal court judge that Carlin has now observed, possess no such grandeur. Barth's robing room is dominated by a single oak desk, circa 1946, which squats in the middle of the room, surrounded by one oak chair and two belching radiators. There is no rug to cover the scuffed brown linoleum, and there are no curtains to frame the dirty windows looking out on a construction site where yet another government office building is going up.

Hands in his pants pockets, Carlin looks out the window at the construction site where two workmen are pouring cement. Carlin appears to be relaxed and fascinated by the workmen; but in his mind, he is countering the arguments he thinks Barth will make to persuade him to offer John Harding a low plea.

Barbara Jennings makes no pretense of being at ease. Standing in front of Barth's desk, she appears as if she has just been hit with one of those headache hammers that aspirin makers love to create for their television commercials. She is squinting and her lips quiver slightly. Barbara Jennings is thinking that her client, John Harding, is already in serious trouble and that he will meet some disastrous fate as a result of this conference.

Barth, who sits in the room's only chair, opens the discussion. "Look, I still think we ought to be able to get a plea in this Harding case," he says. "This trial's a waste of the taxpayer's money and your time. What can you offer the defendant?"

Carlin is silent.

"Bob, this kid is no vicious killer. His record's pretty light—two minor drug counts are the worst of it, I think."

"He's been off heroin for three years," Barbara Jennings interjects. "He hasn't been arrested since. Except for this case."

"This was an impulsive act by a kid who got mad," says Barth. "I don't think he went into that office wanting to hurt Karen Petersen or even to take money from that safe."

"But, Judge, he did it, and Karen Petersen has twenty-eight stitches to prove it," Carlin counters.

"She was out of the hospital the same day," says Barth. "I think it was a symbolic gesture by Harding. He didn't want to kill her. If he'd wanted to, you can be damn sure he could have. Come on, Bob, what can you offer?"

Carlin says nothing.

"What about attempted assault, top of seven?" asks Barth. "That will put Mr. Harding away for a while. That's a lot of time for a twenty-four-year-old kid with no record to speak of."

Barbara Jennings does not offer her advice nor does Barth ask for it. Barth looks straight at Carlin. The Assistant DA evades Barth's stare, looking out the window. "All right," Carlin says finally. "Attempted assault."

"Miss Jennings," Barth says triumphantly, "you've just been offered the bargain of the century. It's an offer I don't think Mr. Harding can refuse."

"I'll speak to my client," she replies.

"Go ahead. We'll wait for you."

Twenty minutes later, Barbara Jennings returns. Barth can see from her downcast expression that she has failed to persuade her client to take the plea.

"Your Honor, Mr. Harding wants to go ahead with the trial," Barbara says, almost inaudibly.

Barth broods silently. John Harding has just balked at the best break he'll probably ever get. And he has rejected the advice of his attorney. Dammit, there ought to be a course in

(23)

law school on how to counsel stubborn defendants. When I was a young lawyer, Bill Logan gave me an invaluable cram course on the subject. It happened back when Logan and I were appointed to defend Tom Stubbs, who was charged with Murder One:

According to five witnesses at the High-Hat Bar, Stubbs had walked into the bar one night and announced that he was going to kill "a no good motherfucker named Sanford" if he caught up with him. An hour later, Stubbs returned to the bar, spotted Sanford there, and shot him dead. After he was arrested, Stubbs confessed and showed the police where he had thrown the gun.

When Barth first interviewed Stubbs, the defendant recounted the entire chain of events with no trace of emotion. Had Sanford threatened him? No. Or intimidated him? No. Had the victim done anything to justify Stubbs's action? No, replied Stubbs calmly. Barth remembered admiring Stubbs's stoicism. Facing the possibility of the electric chair, he wasn't sure he could have pulled off the interview with such aplomb.

But, as plea time approached, Stubbs's memory got increasingly fuzzy. He didn't remember what happened that night in the bar. But he was certain that he hadn't done everything he had confessed to. Finally, he told Barth that he wanted a trial.

As Stubbs explained his decision, Barth's mind raced through possible rebuttal arguments that he might present to his client. He tried every one of them. "Tom," Barth pleaded, "the prosecution's got the strongest possible case. They've got the murder weapon. They've got the witnesses. They've got your confession."

Tom Stubbs just shook his head and said he wanted a trial.

Barth tried again. "Tom, think of your wife and family. If you go to trial and are convicted, you may go to the electric chair. Who'll take care of them? At least, if you take a plea, you'll be alive."

"No," said Stubbs, he would not take a plea.

"Tom," Barth finally said, "I'm not sure in good conscience that I can represent you if you insist on going to trial. I may not be able to give you proper representation feeling, as I do, that you should not go to trial."

Impassively, Stubbs replied that that was Barth's decision. The defendant said that he would let Bill Logan defend him alone, if necessary.

A desperate Barth called Logan and told him about Stubbs's intransigence. Logan said he would come to the jail immediately to talk to Stubbs. Within fifteen minutes, Tom Stubbs was repeating his decision to Logan. After Stubbs had finished, both the defendant and Barth looked at Logan, waiting for him to speak. At first, Logan said nothing. Then, in a quiet and friendly manner, Logan began to talk to Stubbs. "You know, Mr. Stubbs, that the charge against you is Murder One, for which, if convicted, you could be sent to the electric chair. Now we have a lot to talk about in preparing our case for trial. But first, let me take a few minutes to tell you about some of my former clients who, like you, decided to go to trial on a Murder One count rather than take a plea. They were convicted, of course. And they were sent upstate to die in the electric chair. You know how they prepare you for the electric chair, don't you?" asked Logan.

Stubbs, by now demonstrably uncomfortable, shook his head.

"Well, they take you down this long green corridor until you come to this tiny room. The chair, with the straps and wires, is in the middle. Nothing else is in the room. They sit you down and the first thing they do, Mr. Stubbs, is slit your pants and shirt sleeves so they can put the wires on. Then they shave off all of your hair. Hurts a little, but it's necessary, you understand. Makes their job a little easier. Then they strap you down. The first current will lift you clear out of your chair if they don't. Then it starts. *Buzzt.*"

Logan jerked his head back and gave a violent shriek. Tom Stubbs jumped a foot. Logan straightened up and a friendly calm returned to his face. Smiling now, Logan said, "Now, Mr. Stubbs, let's get to your case." He took a deep breath and sighed, "We've got a lot of work to do for your trial."

Tom Stubbs never went to trial. He pleaded guilty to manslaughter. Bill Logan probably saved Stubbs's life with that little story. If Barth alone had been representing Tom Stubbs, the defendant would have gone to trial, would almost certainly have been convicted, and would probably have died in the electric chair.

Most young lawyers today are no different from the way I was twenty-five years ago, Barth says to himself. They are not experienced enough to talk tough to their clients. They are too worried about offending the defendant or making a mistake in judgment. So they go along, which is usually the worst possible thing they can do for their clients.

Barbara Jennings is suffering in the same way I did when I couldn't handle Tom Stubbs. I know her problem well. I wish I could tell her, but that's not my job. She'll learn. Not as quickly as I did, since she does not have Bill Logan for a tutor. But she'll learn.

"All right, let's proceed," Barth says as he rises slowly from his chair. "Barbara, will you please tell Mr. Giles to call in the Harding jury?"

After George Giles announces "The People versus John Harding," Alfred Lorenzo leads Karen Petersen to the witness stand. Barbara Jennings rises for her cross-examination. She takes her handwritten notes to the jury box and sets them down on the wooden railing. She slides her hands in her suit pockets. Her voice is soft and courteous.

"Miss Petersen," Barbara Jennings begins, "have you ever had any unpleasant experiences with black employees?"

"I don't understand what you mean," the witness responds.

"Have you ever had arguments with any of your black employees?"

"No."

"Did you know any blacks in Sweden?"

"No."

"Miss Petersen, were you nervous about living in this city?"

"No."

"Had you heard of racial tensions here?"

Carlin objects to the question as irrelevant.

Sustained.

"Have you ever been a victim of a crime?"

"No."

"Were you angry with John Harding on the days he left without paying back the advances?"

"No."

"Were you upset?"

"Yes," says the witness firmly.

"But you just said you weren't angry."

"There is a difference between being angry and being upset." The witness is in complete control of herself now. Her answers are crisp and to the point. She looks directly at Barbara Jennings as she answers.

Barbara, you're searching for a hostility toward blacks that isn't there, Barth is thinking. Miss Petersen is a Swede. Better move on to something else. Barbara Jennings seems to be reading the judge's mind.

"Miss Petersen, you say that the man who entered your office on the afternoon of June twenty-second demanded money. Is that right?"

(27)

"John asked me for money."

"Miss Petersen, your assailant came up from behind you, isn't that right?"

"Yes."

"And he tied you up and made you lie face down on the floor, isn't that right?"

"Yes."

"Then could you please tell me how you are so sure that your assailant was the defendant?"

"Because I turned around when he put his arm around my neck and I saw John Harding. And when I was tied up and lying on the floor I could still see John Harding."

"Could you please describe the assailant?" asks Miss Jennings. "What was he wearing?"

The witness hesitates. "I don't remember what he was wearing . . ."

Carlin rises. "I object to that question. The witness has already identified the defendant as the man in her office."

Sustained.

"Miss Petersen, who was in your office when your assailant entered?"

"Mrs. Mendoza, my office girl."

Barbara Jennings shuffles through her notes. "Miss Petersen, do you recall your grand jury testimony in which you said that at three fifteen P.M. on June twenty-second Mrs. Mendoza *and* your office girl were in your office?"

"I said Mrs. Mendoza, my office girl," the witness replies instantly. No contradiction there. Silently, Barbara Jennings turns to another page of her notes.

Miss Petersen and Barbara have virtually reversed roles. It is Miss Petersen, the witness, who is scoring points, answering each inquiry in strong, intimidating tones. And it is Barbara, officially the interrogator, who seems uncomfortable, almost devastated, by the responses of her witness. Barbara should have quit a long time ago, Barth reflects. Karen Petersen is too good a witness. She sticks to her story. The only thing left for Barbara to do is to nit-pick. But the more she does it, the more the jury is going to sympathize with Miss Petersen. They're fidgeting already. They're probably asking themselves why this poor woman is being put through her ordeal a second time.

Barbara Jennings tries again to discover weaknesses and contradictions in the witness's story. She is not successful.

The next witness is Mrs. Sara Mendoza, a portly woman in her late forties, dressed in a full lavender skirt and white blouse. She wears thick glasses and speaks in effusive phrases, given dramatic emphasis by the roll of the Spanish *R*.

After Bob Carlin has led Mrs. Mendoza through a series of preliminary questions which place her in the fourteenth-floor cafeteria office next to her boss, Karen Petersen, on the afternoon of June twenty-second, the prosecutor asks the witness to describe what happened.

"There was a terrible noise," says Mrs. Mendoza.

"And when did you hear that noise, Mrs. Mendoza?" asks Carlin.

"It was about three fifteen."

"And what did you do when you heard the noise?"

"I looked up," Mrs. Mendoza responds, her eyes widening in anticipation of what she is about to say. "And I saw John Harding with his arm around Miss Petersen's neck."

"When did you first know that the man in the office was John Harding?" asks Bob.

"I knew it immediately," the witness responds emphatically. "It was John Harding with his arm around Miss Petersen's neck. And he had a knife in his other hand," Mrs. Mendoza adds with a slight shudder.

"You're sure it was John Harding?"

"Oh, yes."

"And what did you do, Mrs. Mendoza?"

"I said, 'John, don't do this. Think of your mother. Think of your father. You are a nice young boy. Don't get into more trouble.' " Mrs. Mendoza places her hands together in a gesture of prayer. "I even got on my knees and pleaded with John. I said, 'Please, John. Don't do this. John, think of your mother. John, think of your father.' "

Barth is thinking: Now this is real theater! Courtroom drama at its best. The jury can visualize poor Mrs. Mendoza on her knees, praying for John Harding's soul. "John, think of your mother. John, think of your father." Terrific.

"And what did John Harding do then?" asks Carlin.

"He told me to shut up. He said, 'Mendoza, shut up.' "

"And what did you do?"

"I shut up."

The witness's answer brings smiles to the jurors' faces.

When it is Barbara Jennings's turn to cross-examine, she desperately searches to find points in Mrs. Mendoza's testimony that conflict with Karen Petersen's. But Mrs. Mendoza remembers the exact time John Harding entered the office that afternoon, the exact time he left, the exact time police officers came. All coincide with the times given by Karen Petersen. When Barbara presses Mrs. Mendoza, she is to regret it.

"When you were tied up and placed on your stomach on the floor, isn't it true that you could not see what the man in the office was doing?"

"I could not see John's face," Mrs. Mendoza replies slowly. "But I knew what he was doing because I saw the blood dripping to the floor." The memory causes the witness to shudder.

"Your Honor, I would ask that that answer be stricken from the record as not being responsive to the question," Barbara Jennings pleads.

(30)

"Overruled."

After the witness has been dismissed, Barth reflects: Barbara should have been more careful with Mrs. Mendoza. Miss Petersen was a good witness; Mrs. Mendoza was even better. There was no sharp edge to her testimony, no arrogance that occasionally crept into Karen Petersen's testimony. Miss Petersen referred to Mrs. Mendoza as her "office girl." Minority members of the jury may not like that. But there was absolutely nothing the jury could dislike about Mrs. Mendoza.

Mrs. Mendoza is followed on the witness stand by Doctor Robert Glazer, the resident at Blauvelt Hospital who treated Karen Petersen on the afternoon of June 22. Dr. Glazer testifies that Karen Petersen was brought to the Emergency Room at approximately four that afternoon, her neck bleeding as a result of a knife wound. The injury required twenty-eight sutures across Miss Petersen's throat, Doctor Glazer says. Barbara Jennings does not challenge the doctor's testimony.

The final witness of the afternoon is Detective John Murphy, a florid-faced veteran of twenty-one years on the city police force. Based on the eyewitness identification supplied to the police by Karen Petersen and Sara Mendoza, Murphy arrested John Harding in his apartment on June 28. Murphy also searched Harding's apartment and found receipts for shoes costing $37 and a gray overcoat priced at $75. The receipts were dated June 22, the day of the assault and robbery in Karen Petersen's office. Murphy produces the receipts and they are entered into evidence.

For the first time that day, Barbara has a weak prosecution witness and she seems to sense it. Her voice is strong as she directs her questions to the witness.

"You testified, Detective Murphy, that you arrested John Harding on June twenty-eighth. Is that correct?"

"Yes."

"Detective Murphy, could you tell the jury when you first

received information on the crime for which you arrested John Harding?"

"Yes, I think it was June twenty-second."

"Now, Detective Murphy, could you tell us why, if you received information on Karen Petersen's assailant on June twenty-second, you waited six full days to make the arrest?"

"I'll be glad to," answers Murphy without hesitation or a trace of defensiveness. "I received the assignment just as I was about to leave work Friday for a five-day vacation. I thought the assignment could wait until I got back. There was no problem with the arrest on the twenty-eighth."

"Detective Murphy, you are saying that the arrest in an assault and armed robbery case was made six days after the assignment. You must have had some doubt about the merit of the arrest? Isn't that the real reason for the delay?"

"Not at all. Like I told you, I had vacation time coming and thought I could complete the assignment when I got back."

Barbara pauses and, in full view of the jury, gives Detective Murphy an incredulous look.

After the witness is dismissed, it is clear that his inept testimony has done wonders for the morale of the defense. It shows in Barbara's full stride back to the defense table. And it shows in John Harding's welcoming smile for his attorney.

"Your Honor," says Bob Carlin, "the prosecution rests."

"May we approach the bench?" asks Barbara.

Barth motions Barbara Jennings and Bob Carlin forward.

"Your Honor," says Barbara, "my first witness won't be available until tomorrow morning. Could we adjourn until then?"

"It is now four forty-five," says Barth, "which means we couldn't get much more testimony in today even if your first witness was ready. I suggest we adjourn until tomorrow morning at eleven. That will give you time to collect your witnesses, Barbara, and it will give me time to take care of other court business before trial. Is that agreeable to both of you?"

The attorneys nod.

After Barth has dismissed the jury for the day, he and George Giles walk to the elevator.

"Barbara really has her hands full with this one, doesn't she, Judge?" says Giles.

"I think so. Bob Carlin presented a strong case. Both Karen Petersen and Mrs. Mendoza were good witnesses. Miss Petersen's story seems credible. And Mrs. Mendoza, on her knees, no less, pleading with John Harding. That's going to be hard for Barbara to match. She did score a few points with her cross-examination of Detective Murphy, but I don't think that will be enough. She'll have to have a strong defense."

"I wonder what her defense will be," says Giles.

"I suspect she's going to put John Harding and one or two members of his family on the stand as alibi witnesses."

"But she waived an opening statement, Judge. I thought if you had an alibi defense, you always said so in an opening statement."

"That's usually the case," Barth replies.

"Do you think Barbara's making a mistake?"

"Well, she doesn't really have much choice. She probably waived her opening statement hoping that she could win an acquittal on the basis of her cross-examination of Carlin's witnesses. But Karen Petersen and Mrs. Mendoza were too strong. So Barbara's only recourse is to put on her own witnesses. Ordinarily, I don't consider it good strategy to put a defendant with a criminal record on the witness stand. But Barbara may prove me wrong."

Barth sits at the dining room table, his napkin stuffed in at the collar, and takes giant bites of his porterhouse steak. A gulp of Heineken's, two forkfuls of his baked potato, and back to the steak. He says nothing.

Helen Barth sits at the other end of the table, quietly picking at her food. She is a woman whose good looks have changed remarkably little since she and Jimmy Barth were in law school together. She still has taut, pale white skin, high cheek bones and auburn hair only slightly flecked with gray. She begins to cast angry, then anxious looks at her husband. Finally, she speaks.

"Jimmy, you haven't said one word since we've sat down to dinner. What's the matter? Is it the Harding trial?"

Barth looks blankly at her, then takes another bite of steak. Still he says nothing.

"It is the Harding case," Helen says, her soft voice rising, putting her husband on notice that she is demanding a response.

Barth wipes his lips with his napkin and pushes his plate toward the center of the table. "You're right," he says. "It's a real stinker. John Harding may well be innocent of cutting Karen Petersen's throat and taking twenty-four hundred dollars from the cafeteria office safe. But I'm damned if I think he and his attorney are going to be able to convince this jury of it. You should have heard the prosecution's witnesses. First, the DA brings in Karen Petersen. She is terrified. But her fear does not prevent her from making an unequivocal identification of John Harding as her attacker. And then her office assistant, a Mrs. Mendoza, comes to the stand and repeats everything that Miss Petersen said, but this time with a Spanish accent and lots of soulful emotion. I think the jury believed them. Frankly, I did."

"Then I don't understand why you're upset. The prosecution has presented a solid case. The jury has heard it and, presumably, after the defense presents its case, will return an honest verdict."

"But that's not the point. I don't think we need to wait on the jury to return a verdict that ties up a courtroom, a judge, a clerk, a court reporter, two attorneys, the jurors, and witnesses for the better part of a week at a cost of thousands of dollars to the taxpayers. The result? To stick young John Harding with a heavy felony conviction. That, in turn, will put pressure on me to give him a much heavier sentence than he would get by taking a plea. He should have taken the plea the DA offered him today. But he turned it down."

"That's not your fault, Jimmy. You're doing your job whether Harding takes a plea or goes to trial."

"I know that," Barth says impatiently. "I also know that I should be happy that Mr. Harding is exercising his constitutional rights to a trial by jury. That means he'll be dealt with in open court, not in plea-bargaining sessions in my robing room. And, according to every Law Day speech I've ever heard, that is a laudable goal. The trouble is that I'm not sure I believe it. I think it would be better in this case for everybody, including Harding, if the defendant would take a plea."

"You sound as if you're more worried about John Harding than that woman who got her throat slit. Do you think she would agree with you that everybody ought to try to save you court time and John Harding prison time?"

"Of course not. And I wouldn't blame her if she wanted to put Harding away for the rest of his life, which, I'm sure, is what she wants to do. But I'm paid to see the case from a different perspective. The important question to me is: How much of a threat does John Harding present to the city's law-abiding citizens? My own judgment is that the threat is very small."

"You're saying that a man who comes into a cafeteria office, slits a woman's throat and takes twenty-four hundred dollars from a safe presents a very small threat to the law-abiding citizens of our city?"

"Let me finish, Helen. If Harding committed the crime, he certainly presented a threat to Karen Petersen last summer and he followed through on that threat. But that only begs the more relevant question for me. Will he do it again? I don't think so, because I don't think John Harding is a hardened criminal. I think he was angry last summer and I think he acted impulsively on that anger."

"That may be true," Helen says. "But I still think he ought to go to prison for a long time. He's done a terrible thing and he ought to be punished for it."

"All right. All right. If Harding did it—and, remember, we still don't know that he did it—he should do state time. But not the kind of time that ought to accompany a conviction of armed robbery in the first degree and assault."

"Jimmy, you want to play all of the parts in your courthouse drama. First, you want to be the attorney who knows the best legal course for the defendant to take. Second, you want to be the defendant and accept the advice of the attorney. Third, if the defendant turns down a plea, you want to be the jury and decide who is telling the truth and who isn't. And finally, you want to be yourself, the judge, who is above the battle and can make some sense and 'justice' out of it all. Well, I personally think you take on too much responsibility for yourself."

Barth bends his head down for a moment, as he usually does before responding to one of Helen's challenges. When he looks up, he says, "I took this job, in part, because I thought it would give me power to make things happen in court that I couldn't

(36)

control as a trial lawyer. But the frustrations are still there. This Harding trial is a perfect example. Here I think I have a firm idea of what the best solution to the case ought to be, and the defendant, a twenty-four-year-old high school dropout, vetoes my grand plan." Barth adds, smiling now, "It doesn't seem fair."

"It does to me, Jimmy," says Helen, with just the touch of sympathy in her voice necessary to make Barth forget about the Harding trial and ask her about her day counseling clients on their tax problems at the law firm of Hastings and Hastings.

II
Tuesday

8:32 A.M.

Barth stares at the stack of manila folders on his desk. They are fat with typed probation reports, xeroxed criminal records, and scribbled notes that Barth has written himself about these defendants whom he must judge this morning before presiding over the Harding trial. He picks up the first folder. Martin Johnson, twenty-five, has been charged with the vicious rapes and robberies of three women. It is not Barth's choice of cases to start the morning with. . . .

The time was 2:30 on a drizzily November morning. Amy Lee Ballard was returning to her apartment after working as an operator on the night shift at the telephone company. She stepped into the empty apartment elevator and pressed the button for the sixth floor. As the elevator door was closing, a stocky man wearing a brown leather jacket, and later identified by Amy Lee Ballard as Martin Johnson, squeezed through the door. The woman immediatley sensed trouble and tried to escape. But Johnson blocked her path with his thick body.

When the elevator door had closed tightly, Johnson opened his coat, quickly pulled out a butcher knife, and announced, "I'm gonna have you, woman, or I'm gonna kill you."

Johnson kept his finger on the "close" button while the elevator passed the sixth floor. When it stopped at the eighth floor, he ordered Amy Lee Ballard out and directed her up the stairs to the roof landing.

"Please don't," the woman whimpered, "please don't do this to me."

Martin Johnson said nothing but continued to shove the woman up the stairs. The landing was dark and deserted as the two figures, one after the other, stumbled to the northeast edge.

"Okay, woman," said Johnson, "pull down my pants and suck my dick."

Amy Lee Ballard shook her head and cried, "No, please, no, no."

Johnson pushed her to the ground and grabbed her by the neck. "Woman," he yelled, "it's my dick or your neck."

Slowly, painfully, Amy Lee Ballard unbuttoned Martin Johnson's blue jeans and did what she was told.

"That's better," said Johnson, breathing heavily.

She sucked tentatively at first and, then, when Johnson shouted, "Harder," more vigorously. When the organ began to harden in Amy Ballard's mouth, she was told to take it out.

"Take off your clothes," shouted Johnson, panting.

She hesitated, but when Johnson brandished his knife in front of her, she began to peel off her clothes. She dropped her skirt and blouse, then her bra and panties in a pile next to her. Shivering and naked, Amy Lee Ballard was told to lie down on the wet concrete landing.

"Please, let me go," she pleaded.

"I said to lie down," said Johnson. "Now do it."

The woman kneeled on the concrete and turned her face toward Johnson and the constant drizzle.

"Lie down and spread your legs," he shouted.

Between sobs and whines, Amy Lee Ballard moved her body into position for intercourse. Johnson fell to his knees, forced himself inside of his victim and began pumping with a short frenetic motion. Within forty-five seconds, he had come to orgasm and was slouched on top of the trembling female body.

"Please let me go now," sobbed Amy Lee Ballard. "Please, please, let me go."

"Not yet, woman," groaned Johnson, rising to his feet. "Where's your money?"

Suddenly, Amy Ballard grabbed her pocketbook, which was lying beside her skirt. "Here, take everything," she shrieked. "Take it all." She threw the purse at Johnson and then lunged at her attacker, clawing at his eyes. Johnson gave her three quick punches to the face and a kick in the abdomen. Then, he stuffed six one-dollar bills from her purse into his pants pocket and ran away.

Five days later, a man subsequently identified as Martin Johnson walked into Lorraine's Restaurant, located two blocks away from Amy Lee Ballard's apartment building. The time was 12:15 A.M. and the owner, Lorraine Kelton, was closing up for the night. Armed with a butcher knife, Johnson forced Mrs. Kelton to the floor, ripped off her clothes, and raped her. Before leaving with a television set and $76 from the cash register, Johnson cut Mrs. Kelton on the forehead. The cut required ten stitches.

Two weeks after the attack in Lorraine's Restaurant, a man identified as Martin Johnson accosted Susan Moorhead, a sophomore at the city's community college, as Miss Moorhead was walking to her apartment from the college library. At knife point, Miss Moorhead was pushed into an alley and forced to have intercourse with her attacker. Afterward, Johnson took $4.25 from the victim's wallet, punched her in the face, and fled.

Barth grimaces as he turns the page of Johnson's report to review the defendant's prior criminal record. It extends to four full, single-spaced typewritten pages. In 1965 Martin Johnson was arrested for petty larceny and released to his mother's custody (his father left home when Johnson was three). In 1966 Johnson was arrested for the assault of a sixteen-year-old girl, but the case was dismissed. In 1967 Johnson was given a suspended sentence after being convicted of possession of heroin. He was next arrested and convicted in 1969 for the assault and robbery of a female proprietor of a restaurant and served two years in the state penitentiary. Eighteen months ago, Johnson had been charged with rape, but was acquitted by a jury. Three months later, he was again arrested as a prime suspect in a rape case, but charges were later dropped.

When Johnson had appeared before Barth a month ago, Barth had become familiar with the defendant's criminal activities. He also knew that Johnson came from a broken home, had dropped out of school in the seventh grade, possessed no skill, and had never held a steady job. A psychiatric report said that Johnson was insecure but not insane. Reading the police report, Barth strongly suspected that Martin Johnson was guilty of the crimes he had been charged with. None of the three victims hesitated in identifying Johnson as her attacker. In addition, a passer-by, who heard the screams of Lorraine Kelton in her restaurant, had rushed in and chased the attacker just as he was leaving the restaurant. The witness later identified Martin Johnson as the man he had chased out of Lorraine's Restaurant.

A strong case against Johnson but not, Barth knew, an easy one for the prosecution. First of all, rape trials take an incalculable toll on the victims, assuming that the victims testify, which is never certain until they are on the witness stand. Amy Lee Ballard, Lorraine Kelton, and Susan Moorhead were certain that Martin Johnson attacked them last November, but as the time for trial approached, their memories might fade as their fears mounted. And proving rape primarily on the basis of testimony of the victims, no matter how strong, was never easy. Barth was also worried about the case because young John Thompson in the DA's office had been assigned to prosecute. Barth was not certain that Thompson, new to the DA's office last fall, could handle such a heavy case.

For all of these reasons, Barth had decided in that plea-bargaining session a month ago that he would push very hard for Martin Johnson to take a plea. After a series of consultations between Johnson and his legal aid attorney, Arthur Kandell, the defendant agreed to plead guilty to one count of armed robbery if he were promised a sentence below the maximum of twenty-five years. Barth promised that he would sentence the defendant to a top of eighteen years and that he would make his promise a part of the record when Johnson took the plea. Martin Johnson had taken the plea in Barth's courtroom last month, much to Barth's relief. Putting Johnson away for that length of time, Barth felt, was rendering a considerable community service.

But Martin Johnson had undergone a change of heart sometime between last month's plea and this Tuesday morning when he is scheduled to be sentenced. According to the presentencing report, Martin Johnson "now denies his guilt. He states that he pleaded guilty on advice of counsel and because he felt it was in his own best interest. But he desires that his plea of guilty remain."

Barth ponders the problem. Johnson wants it both ways. He wants to take his plea while he maintains his innocence. If he decides later to press his claim of innocence, the state court of appeals might rule that the defendant's plea had been coerced and, therefore, that Martin Johnson had been denied due process of law in my courtroom. I don't like to be reversed by the appellate court, but I like even less being manipulated by a vicious rapist like Martin Johnson. I'm not playing Johnson's game. When he comes in today, I'm going to put everything on the record and I'm still going to sentence the son of a bitch to eighteen years.

The folder of Tillie Martin is back on Barth's desk. This time she has pleaded guilty to the charge of attempted murder. Poor Tillie. Barth knows her pitiful history well. She has been in and out of mental institutions for the last twenty years. This time she got into serious trouble, stabbing a man she calls her "boyfriend" and very nearly killing him. Apparently, only Tillie took the love relationship seriously. The "boyfriend" has denied any amorous tie.

According to Tillie, the incident took place last summer after she received word from Martians that she alone could save President John F. Kennedy. She thought her "boyfriend" was threatening JFK, so she stabbed him with a kitchen knife. When police arrived, there was Tillie covered with her victim's blood, muttering that she was defending the late President Kennedy.

Tillie Martin's new psychiatric report reads pretty much as Barth expects. She has a long history of psychotic illness. She is diagnosed as a paranoid-schizophrenic continually under delusions that her life is in danger. I have no reason to doubt the analysis or the need for intensive psychiatric treatment for Tillie, Barth reflects. I have a problem, however, that has to do with the technicalities of the law. If I find Tillie legally insane today, she will be committed, still facing a trial once she is judged mentally competent. I don't think the interests of Tillie or the state will be served by dragging the case out like that. On the other hand, if I find Tillie insane only at the time of her attempted murder, I can close the case and still get Tillie committed. Regardless of the psychiatrist's testimony at the hearing this morning, I'm going to find Tillie insane only at the time of the attempted murder. It's a minor ruse on my part, but one I think will do no one any harm.

Why do I seem to have more compassion for a Tillie Martin, who stabs a "boyfriend," than a Martin Johnson, who attacks young women? If I were asked that question, I guess I would say that Tillie is totally helpless, naked before the law. There is very little anybody, including Tillie herself, can do to help her. So I try to soothe the pain in small ways that reach out to Tillie and, at the same time, protect the public's interest. It's not the same with Martin Johnson. He has problems, sure, but he's not helpless. In reaching out to Mr. Johnson, I may forget about Johnson's next victim. That's a mistake.

Barth picks up the folder of Richard Leone, a defendant whom Barth instinctively files into his category of dangerous characters. Mr. Leone makes his living as a stickup man, and, this time, the police have him cold. He robbed a drugstore at gunpoint and made a clean sweep of the barbiturates. Unfortunately, for Leone, the druggist and two customers watched him do it.

Leone's record includes convictions for armed robbery, assault, possession of drugs, and grand larceny. Barth thumbs to the back of the probation report where the probation officer lists the "mitigating circumstances" that might suggest leniency in treating the defendant. "Leone is currently being treated for drug addiction at Sunshine House Drug Rehabilitation Center," Barth reads. "Robert Kingston, the director of Sunshine House, reports that Leone is making good progress. Kingston says that Leone has been extremely cooperative with his staff and shows signs of finally breaking his habit. The director has recommended that Leone's case be deferred and that he be paroled to Sunshine House for further treatment."

Barth is suspicious. Leone knows that he's going to have problems if he goes to trial. He also knows that, with his record and the present charges, things may not go that well when his attorney, Henry Simpson, and the DA come up to discuss a plea. One way for Leone to help himself is to show that he has made some effort toward rehabilitation. So he goes to Sunshine House. He takes his methadone dutifully and is nice to everybody. Nothing wrong with that. The trouble will come later, Barth speculates, when Richard Leone is pronounced "cured," comes back to court, takes a plea, and is given the expected probationary sentence. Even if Leone is off drugs, he'll go back to his old habits that he had before he ever got into drugs. He'll hurt people. I just don't think I want to be a part of that, Barth concludes.

Before going to his courtroom, Barth briefs himself on what he considers a "garbage" case requiring little of his or anybody else's time. It involves Charles "Ace" Barrett and several other young men, including the complainant, who were playing basketball at St. Nicholas School playground a few months ago. The complainant jokingly remarked that "Ace" had a striking resemblance to a bulldog that paraded past them. Barrett was not amused. In fact, he was so unamused that he went to his car, returned with a .22-caliber revolver tucked in his belt, and wondered if anyone still thought he bore the resemblance to the bulldog. When the complainant insisted on the comparison, Barrett shoved him, pulled his gun, and fired two shots into the air. Police arrived and arrested Barrett for assault and illegal possession of a gun.

Barth reads the probation department's pre-pleading report on Barrett, which tells him that the defendant is "a bad-tempered individual with inappropriate responses to certain situations. Given his size and weight, his potential for violence does seem all the more dangerous."

Barth shakes his head. That probation officer has picked up the jargon of the trade but that's about all. To be sure, Mr.

Charles "Ace" Barrett, like thousands of other dudes who pack Saturday Night Specials, is more dangerous than somebody without a gun. But is Barrett the real problem or do we look to the legislators who won't outlaw guns and the movie producers who make every two-bit gunslinger into a hero?

Now the lawmakers and "model citizens" of Hollywood expect me to do their dirty work for them. They've handed "Ace" Barrett his gun and now they say to me, "Judge Barth, you do something about it." Well, what am I supposed to do? Send Mr. Barrett away for three or four years because he lost his temper and drew a gun instead of a peace sign? I don't think that's going to do anybody any good. Barrett will simply smolder upstate, listening to his fellow inmates tell him that he's a victim of a racist society. And he'll also be told that as long as he's going to do time he might as well aim a little higher. Next time it'll be armed robbery or worse.

Barth now gets down to the business of deciding what to do with Barrett. He has no criminal record. He and a friend got in a fight and Barrett overreacted. Nobody was hurt. It's not something I want to encourage but, then again, I don't want to make too much of it either. Barrett should get off with a fine. With the fine, Barrett will feel that he's been given a fair shake. As a result, other citizens may be less likely in the future to peer at Mr. Barrett from the wrong end of his .22-caliber pistol.

9:30 A.M.

"Are there any lawyers ready to proceed?" Clerk George Giles bellows. No response. Giles pushes his 200 pounds up from his chair and moves over to the bench where Barth is silently brooding.

"You know, Judge, we can use the supermarket approach," says Giles, a devilish grin coming to his face. "Today, shoppers, we have a special on attempted robberies. Five, count 'em, five attempted robberies, top of ten months. This is a special, shoppers, you can't afford to pass up."

Barth brightens. "Don't laugh, George. I knew a judge a few years ago who once did something like that. It was June and he was hot and, I guess, pretty fed up. So he announced that he had two misdemeanors to give away. One defense attorney took him up on the offer and the DA went along. It was a garbage case anyway." Barth pauses. Then, he says, "You know why nobody's ready, don't you, George?"

Giles says nothing.

"It's because nobody wants to be in this courtroom," says Barth. "Young assistant district attorneys are waiting for their big chance with a Murder One trial and don't want to be bothered with these pleas. Defense attorneys can make more money soliciting business someplace else. Pleas mean work for court reporters and boredom for court officers. Defendants? They sure don't want to be here. I guess only Mrs. Murphy over there genuinely looks forward to my calendar."

At 9:39, Melvin Rich, fifty, Barth's balding legal assistant, walks briskly to the front of the bench. As usual, Rich is the best-dressed man in the courtroom, today nattily attired in a three-piece Hart, Schaffner and Marx gray-plaid suit, maroon tie and matching pocket handkerchief. A substantial portion of Rich's salary is spent on clothes; a substantial portion of Rich's time is spent worrying about his job and his boss.

"What's doing, Melvin?" Barth asks.

Rich frowns, as he always does when Barth asks him for information. "Judge Wallace still has the Norris homicide and Judge Gordon will be instructing the jury in the Lowd case," Rich says.

"So they're keeping busy," Barth says.

Rich nods.

That's good, Barth thinks to himself. Since John Talbert asked me to assign cases to Wallace and Gordon, it's been one headache after another. Particularly with Gordon. All that I've heard about him from other lawyers and judges is now confirmed. Judge Jack Gordon seems to have transferred all of his private neuroses into public causes. He rants at any poor slob he thinks is challenging him. The attorneys tell me that includes themselves as well as clerks, court officers, reporters and witnesses. Now he's started on me, screaming that I'm purposely giving him too little to do to make him look bad. Each time he says he's got nothing to do, I point out that he still has control of more than a dozen cases. But that doesn't seem to make an impression. The next time he starts in on me, I'm going to teach Judge Gordon a lesson. He is going to discover that he cannot bully Jimmy Barth.

Barth has now been on the bench for more than fifteen minutes, shuffling his index cards of pending cases. Waiting. This is an utter waste of time, he grumbles. My clerk is here, my court officers are here, my legal assistant is here. Everybody's ready but the goddamn lawyers who won't get off their asses and move the calendar. Finally, he runs out of patience.

"Mr. Giles," Barth says, "will you please begin to call the calendar."

"We'll now proceed with the calendar," Giles announces hopefully.

It doesn't work. The handful of lawyers in the courtroom ignore the call.

"Mr. Giles," booms Barth, unmistakably annoyed. "I think the attorneys need an interpreter. They do not seem to understand English. Would you please find out what language they *do* understand so that we can get on with our business?"

At that moment, a short, stubby white man with slicked-back brown hair and a taller, muscular black companion rise and walk forward. Barth scowls. J. Randall Farr, mouthpiece for a generation of small-time hoods and their friends, has arrived. After Farr has conferred with George Giles

(51)

for thirty seconds, Giles says, "Judge, we can take case number two on the calendar, Charles Barrett." At Farr's direction, Charles "Ace" Barrett sits down at the defense table.

"May we approach, Judge?" Farr asks.

Barth motions Farr and Assistant District Attorney John Thompson, the "catcher" for the DA's office in Barth's courtroom this morning, to the bench. With his short brown hair, thick glasses, and slight hint of acne, Thompson looks like the vice-president of the local Methodist youth group.

"Mr. Farr," Barth asks, "what does your client do for a living?"

"He's a basketball player," Farr replies.

"That's very nice, but what does he do for a living?"

"I'm serious, Judge. He plays semipro ball. His team's going to Mexico next week."

Barth takes a look at the defendant's impressive physique. The basketball story is believable. Playing semipro ball could keep Mr. Barrett out of trouble. Besides, that playground argument that got him into this mess isn't worth wasting courtroom time on.

"Mr. Thompson," Barth says, "this is a nothing case. Are you agreeable to a misdemeanor?"

Thompson is agreeable.

"I don't want to put him on probation," Barth says, thinking out loud. "That'll interrupt his employment. Gentlemen, make me an offer."

"A two hundred and fifty dollar fine," says Farr instantly.

"Sold."

Thompson returns to the prosecutor's table, and Farr, with a big quarter-moon smile on his face, walks over to Barrett to tell him the good news.

The defendant stands up.

"Mr. Barrett," says Barth. "You are pleading guilty to attempted possession of a dangerous weapon, a misdemeanor. Do you understand that."

Barrett nods.

"That means that you are admitting that you, in fact, did attempt to possess a twenty-two caliber revolver at the St. Nicholas School playground on June 22, 1973. Do you understand?"

"Yes."

"Mr. Barrett, I could send you to jail, but I'm not going to do it. I don't think you belong in jail. You have no criminal record. Your attorney, Mr. Farr, tells me you have a steady job as a semipro basketball player."

Barrett nods.

"Let me say one more thing," Barth adds. "This is the last time you'll appear before me for sentence and not go to jail. You get into trouble again and, I promise you, Mr. Barrett, you'll do state time. The sentence of the court is a two hundred and fifty dollar fine."

Barth's eyes follow two figures that are entering the courtroom. The first through the door is a brisk little man, forty perhaps, who is wearing a three-piece suit, rimless glasses, and a nervous smile on his face. Barth nods in recognition of Henry Simpson, Esq. That must be Mr. Leone behind Henry. Leone who is charged with armed robbery of a drugstore, towers over Simpson, Esq. That must be Mr. Leone behind Henry. Leone, that stretches from the left side of his mouth to his left ear. He is dressed neatly in a light beige sport coat, brown slacks, and a white shirt opened at the collar.

The Leone case is called and Henry Simpson marches to the bench.

"Mr. Simpson, what can I do for you today?" asks Barth.

Simpson grins. "My client is in Sunshine House, Judge. If

you could give him a deferred sentence for, say, six months, I think he could complete his treatment."

"Henry, the cops got him dead. It was a stickup of a drugstore. Mr. Leone is thirty-one years old. He has a long sheet. He is no longer an impressionable youth who has gone astray."

Simpson enjoys the judge's analysis or, at least, lets it appear that he does. But he persists. "Your Honor, Mr. Leone has made a remarkable change in the few months that he's been at Sunshine House. He's finally faced his drug problem. He's doing well there. If he could be given a deferred sentence and paroled to Sunshine House, he could complete his treatment. That's all we're asking."

"I don't blame you. It's the best possible course for Leone, given the spot that he's in. The problem is that Mr. Leone is a stickup man. And I don't think a stickup man should be paroled to Sunshine House."

"Judge, I think you're being too cynical in this case," Simpson says.

"I don't think so," Barth replies. "Both Leone and Sunshine House may benefit from Leone's stay there. The problem comes when you put a hood like Leone, who was a stickup man long before he was an addict, back in the real world after his treatment."

Simpson is annoyed. "Judge, I think you're being unfair to Leone and to Sunshine House. They're acting in good faith."

"Look, Mr. Simpson, I am not impressed just because Sunshine House supports Mr. Leone's candidacy. How else will they continue to receive government funds if they don't have clients? As for Mr. Leone's sudden change of heart, this doesn't surprise me either. It's a good deal for him. He's facing a tough rap, so he goes to Sunshine House for a few months and behaves himself. When he returns to court, he'll cop a plea and figures he'll be put on probation. It makes sense for Mr. Leone.

It makes sense for Sunshine House. The only person it doesn't make sense for is Mr. Leone's next victim."

Up to this point, Assistant District Attorney Thompson has not intervened. Now he speaks up. "Your Honor, I agree with you. Leone has a long record. We've got a strong case. I'll let him plead to attempted robbery. But I can't recommend parole."

Barth looks directly at Henry Simpson. "If I put him on parole and he stays at Sunshine House, it is possible that we may see the complete rehabilitation of Richard Leone. But, Mr. Simpson, I'm just cynical enough to think he'll hang around Sunshine House only as long as it serves his purposes. If he takes a plea and gets sentenced to probation, he'll go back to sticking up drugstores. Mr. Leone has to learn there is a price he must pay for his stickups. I'm not going to parole him. Let him plead to attempted armed robbery, top of fifteen. He'll get less."

"Please, Your Honor. Take a chance. Let my client continue in the program at Sunshine House."

"I can't do it. The best I can do, if he doesn't want to take the plea, is to assign him to another judge for trial."

Simpson turns and walks back to the counsel table to confer with Leone. As Barth waits for Leone's decision, he thinks to himself: Maybe I shouldn't take such a hard line. Conceivably, Sunshine House could do wonders for Leone. But I don't like what I've heard about that place. The staff substitutes methadone for heroin and then brags that the customers are cured. All that has really been done is to substitute one habit for another. But even assuming Sunshine House can get Leone away from all drugs, I still can't take a chance on him. He's a stickup man and he's dangerous. The DA's got an easy conviction here. If Henry and his client have any sense, they'll take the plea. Here comes Henry. Let's see what happens.

(55)

"Your Honor, Mr. Leone doesn't want to take the plea, so I guess we'd better set a date for trial," says Simpson.

Barth reaches for his calendar and says, "How about next Monday? I'll give it to Judge Wallace. All right?"

Henry Simpson is not enthusiastic but nods his head affirmatively. He takes out his notebook and marks Monday's date. Assistant DA John Thompson almost salivates in anticipation. "See you Monday, Mr. Simpson," he says.

"Judge, can we take case number three, Tillie Martin?" asks Giles.

Here comes Tillie, the defendant who stabbed her "boyfriend." Her 300-pound body is covered by a tentlike blue striped dress and her lips are heavy with purple lipstick. Her eyes have a dazed look, heightened by thick green eye shadow. When she spots Barth, Tillie smiles and waves at him. Barth waves back, as he would to an old friend, which is what he considers Tillie to be.

Yes, Barth feels that he and Tillie go back a few years. Actually, Barth has only seen Tillie twice, both brief pre-sentencing court sessions. But he feels a special tie to Tillie. Maybe it's because she, more than his other defendants, seems peculiarly vulnerable. He knows her family background and her traumas, what she tells her "boyfriends" and psychiatrists. Unfortunately, though he may care for Tillie, as a doctor would care for his patient, Barth cannot cure her or even be confident that others in the system might. All that he can do is try, in a modest way, to soften the pain. And that is exactly what he intends to do.

Tillie Martin's attorney calls a psychiatrist to the witness stand who testifies that Tillie could not have been criminally responsible for the stabbing of her "boyfriend" because she was mentally ill at the time of the crime. He recounts Tillie's twenty-year history of mental illness and concludes she is a paranoid-schizophrenic who believes her life is continually in danger.

The psychiatrist's testimony is identical to the analysis in Tillie's pre-sentencing report that Barth has read earlier this morning. Twenty seconds after the psychiatrist leaves the witness stand, finds Tillie not guilty of the charge of attempted murder because of her mental condition at the time of the crime. As a result of Barth's ruling, Tillie will not have to stand trial on this charge if and when she is released from the mental hospital. Barth directs that Tillie Martin be immediately committed. He and Tillie then exchange a second round of smiles and waves before she is taken away.

The morning calendar is cleared of all but one item, the sentencing of Martin Johnson, the defendant charged with the rapes and armed robberies of three women, who last month pleaded guilty to one count of armed robbery. Aside from court officers, prosecutor John Thompson, and Johnson's attorney, Arthur Kandell, only the faithful Mrs. Murphy remains in the courtroom.

"Your Honor, I've been down to talk to Martin Johnson," says Kandell, a veteran legal aid attorney whom Barth likes and respects. "He now says he's not guilty of the armed robbery charge. I've checked the minutes and there is nothing in the court record but his plea. I'm worried about an appeal."

"That's all right," Barth replies. "I'll take care of it." He turns to his clerk. "Mr. Giles, call the Johnson case."

A few minutes later, Court Officer Sam Mitchell pushes a wheelchair carrying Martin Johnson into the courtroom. The defendant's right leg is propped up in a cast directly in front of him. His head is down and his right hand covers his right eye. With his head still down, Johnson listens as George Giles reads the charge of armed robbery in the first degree to which he has pleaded guilty.

"Do the People want to be heard prior to sentence?" asks Giles.

"No," Thompson replies.

"Mr. Kandell, do you wish to be heard prior to sentence?" asks Giles.

"Your Honor, I have an application that I wish to submit," says Kandell. "The defendant, Martin Johnson, says that he doesn't want to withdraw his plea of guilty. But he also says he did not commit the crime he has pleaded guilty to. In view of Mr. Johnson's statement made since his plea, that he is not guilty of the crime he pleaded to, I would ask that his plea of guilty be withdrawn and the case go to trial."

Barth rejects Kandell's application without explanation and orders Giles to continue the formal sentencing procedure. Giles asks Johnson if he wants to make a statement.

Johnson lifts his head slowly and begins to speak, although his left eye is shut and he continues to cover the right. "I would like to be sentenced," the defendant says haltingly. "I want to go back to the hospital and get this leg taken care of and do whatever time I should do."

"Do you understand the plea of guilty that you have taken?" asks Giles.

"I . . . understand . . . the . . . plea," the defendant replies.

Arthur Kandell asks to be heard.

Barth nods.

"Your Honor, this defendant has suffered a great deal," says Kandell. "He has lost the sight of one eye. He has lost the movement in one leg. I ask that the court take into consideration the defendant's suffering in sentencing him."

You're right, Arthur, Barth is thinking. Martin Johnson has suffered. Nobody could be as vicious as he's been without having suffered in his own right. If Johnson were analyzed by a competent psychiatrist, I feel confident he would find that Johnson is a profoundly maladjusted young man. I also think that Johnson was fully in control of his faculties when he raped and robbed Amy Lee Ballard, Lorraine Kelton, and Susan Moorhead.

Without changing his stern expression, Barth addresses Kandell and his client. "This defendant was brought here on very serious charges. He was indicted for the vicious rapes and robberies of three innocent women. The victims were prepared to testify against the defendant in court, as was an eyewitness to one of the crimes."

Barth looks directly at Martin Johnson, who now is staring at the empty top of the defense table. "It is hard to say that the defendant didn't deserve what has happened to him. His leg injury was the result of a wound which he inflicted on himself while awaiting disposition of this case. His eye was put out because one of his victims defended her life by poking it out. At the time the defendant sustained his eye injury, he had forced his victim at knife point to take off her clothes and had raped her. So it is a little difficult, I think, to be concerned with the defendant's suffering, since it was brought on by his own acts.

"By sentencing this defendant today, I believe that I am rendering a community service. I am taking him out of society. The sentence of the court is a maximum of eighteen years in the state penitentiary."

11:05 A.M.

A tot the color of dark chocolate sits in the first row of the courtroom seats, clinging fearfully to his mother's left arm. But his mother, trim and handsome in a yellow cotton dress, appears oblivious of his grasp. She continues talking intensely to a female companion, her teeth flashing anger. Her conversation is interrupted by George Giles, who announces, "The People versus John Harding."

Barbara Jennings rises to announce that the first witness for the defense will be Althea Harding. With the announcement, the woman in the yellow cotton dress walks to the witness stand. She takes the oath in a sullenly defiant voice. And then she glowers—at Barth, at Assistant District Attorney Bob Carlin, and at the jury.

Barbara Jennings addresses her witness courteously. "Mrs. Harding, can you tell us where you were on the day of June 22, 1973?" she asks.

"Yes, I can," the witness replies firmly. "I remember that day because it was our son's birthday."

"Please tell the jury what you did that day," Barbara says quietly.

"I wanted to get my little boy a birthday cake. So I called John and asked him to come over and baby-sit for our son, James, while I went out and bought a cake."

"That is John Harding, your husband, isn't it?"

"Yes."

"Mrs. Harding, would you please tell the jury why you and your husband, John Harding, live apart?"

"We can't afford to live together. It's cheaper to live with our families."

"When did you call John Harding on Friday, June twenty-second, and ask him to come over to your apartment?" asks Barbara.

"It was about ten o'clock that morning."

"And when did he come over?"

"Maybe fifteen minutes after I called."

"John Harding came to your apartment at about ten fifteen that morning?"

"That's right."

"And then what did you do?"

"I told John to watch James while I went out to buy a birthday cake. Then I took the bus to the bakery and bought the cake."

"And when did you return to the apartment?"

"About an hour later."

"So you returned to your apartment about eleven fifteen. Is that correct?"

"Yes."

"Was John Harding in the apartment when you returned?"

"Yes, he was."

"Was anybody else in the apartment?"

"Our boy."

"Now, Mrs. Harding, what happened after you returned with the cake to the apartment?"

"I called my sister and told her to bring her kids to the party."

"What was John Harding doing at this time?"

"Playing with James."

"What time was the party?"

"Three o'clock."

"What did you do between the time you invited people to James's party and three o'clock?"

"I set the places for the party. Then I watched TV."

"Did John Harding leave your apartment at any time between eleven fifteen and three o'clock?"

"No."

"You're sure of that?"

"Yes."

"Did anybody else come to your apartment that morning or afternoon before the party?"

"No."

"Did John Harding do anything else besides watch television and play with James before the party?"

"No."

"What time did your sister and her children arrive for the party?"

"At three o'clock."

"Mrs. Harding, how did you know it was three o'clock?"

"Because we were watching television and that's the time 'Another World' comes on. I remember turning off the television when that show came on. That's when my sister came."

"How long did the party last?"

"Until four o'clock."

"How did you know it was four o'clock?"

"That's when 'Somerset' comes on. I remember that the party was over and John and I were watching 'Somerset.' "

"The party lasted from three o'clock until four o'clock on June twenty-second, is that right?"

"Yes."

"And John Harding was at the party the entire time, from three until four. Is that right?"

"That's right."

"Who else was at the party, Mrs. Harding?"

"James and myself and my sister, Diane Smith, and her two little girls."

"Is that all?"

"Yes."

"Were all of you in your apartment from three o'clock until four o'clock?"

"Yes."

"And did anybody at the party have to leave your apartment from three o'clock until four o'clock for any reason?"

"No."

"What did John Harding do at the party?"

"He played with James and the other kids. And he cut the cake."

"Anything else?"

"I don't think so."

"Did John Harding stay in your apartment after the party?"

"Yes."

"How long did he stay at your apartment that day, Mrs. Harding?"

"All afternoon and evening. John didn't go home until about eleven o'clock."

"You are saying, then, that John Harding came to your apartment at ten fifteen A.M. on June twenty-second, and that he was there the entire day and did not leave until about eleven that night. Is that right?"

"That's right."

"And you're sure of that."

"Yes."

We have now heard the standard television alibi, Barth is thinking. Mrs. Harding tells time by the television schedule, not a watch. It's not so far-fetched. Television and drugs are about the only tranquilizers available to the poor. Whether a predominantly white, middle-class jury is going to believe the television alibi is another matter.

If I were Bob Carlin, I would handle Althea Harding with extreme care. She doesn't like any of us and what we are doing to her and her husband. Her hostility could explode at any minute. She could take out after me or Carlin or all of us who represent the white establishment. And if she does, she'll probably touch a sensitive nerve in at least one of the three black jurors. No, Bob Carlin will do well to keep his questions and Althea Harding's answers short and to the point.

Bob Carlin walks slowly to the railing in front of the jury, holding his notes in his hands. He stares at Althea Harding, without speaking. The witness meets the prosecutor's eyes with a steady glare.

"You testified that you called John Harding the morning of June twenty-second to tell him about your son's birthday party?"

"Yes."

"Didn't John Harding know when his son's birthday was?"

"Yes, he did."

"Then why did you have to call on his son's birthday to tell him about it?"

"I told him about the party. I wasn't telling him it was James's birthday."

"Is there any reason that you waited until the morning of your son's birthday before deciding to have a party?"

"No, I just wanted to have a party and decided to that morning."

"And John learned about it that morning?"

"That's right."

"You said John Harding came to your apartment about ten fifteen the morning of June twenty-second, is that right?"

"Yes."

"How did you know it was ten fifteen?"

"Because I was watching 'Romper Room' when John came in. It's on from ten to ten thirty."

"And you say that you took a bus to a bakery to get a cake. What bakery was it?"

"Laird's."

"Mrs. Harding, why did you take a bus? Wasn't there a bakery nearby?"

"Laird's is the closest."

"You live with your mother, don't you, Mrs. Harding?"

"Yes, I do."

"Did you tell your mother about the birthday party?"

"No," the witness replies curtly. "My mother and I aren't speaking."

"Where was your mother when the party was going on?"

"She was out."

"Do you know where she was?"

"No."

(64)

"Was your mother in the apartment during the day?"

"No."

"Was she there at any time when John Harding was there?"

"No, she left early in the morning and didn't come back until late, after John left."

"I have no further questions," says Bob.

Barth watches Althea Harding stalk out of the courtroom. Mrs. Harding is one cool customer, he is thinking. Tough and proud and defiant. Carlin was smart to handle her with care. She knew her story and she knew the TV schedule, and Bob could not change either one.

1:06 P.M.

Barth is late for his luncheon meeting, and his tardiness, he suspects, is the handiwork of his subconscious mind. On the first Tuesday of every month, the judges of his jurisdiction meet over leathery roast beef and mashed potatoes to discuss common problems and grievances. Such meetings, Barth lectures himself regularly, are necessary to the smooth operation of General Motors, Harvard University, and, presumably, Guru Maharaj Ji's march to spiritual peace. Like the other members of organized society, judges ought to be given the opportunity every month or so to fall in love, once again, with the sounds of their own voices.

As Barth enters the ninth-floor dining room, he spots the familiar vases of red roses on the long, narrow dining table. His colleagues are still milling about, which means that the meeting has not started, a conclusion that Barth arrives at with a mixture of relief and disappointment. He stands on the outer edge of an informal circle of judges and tries to look interested in their conversation. Judge David Walker reports on his fractured wrist and the largest bill in medical history. Judge Edward Barnard begins a capsule analysis of a local law journal

(65)

article on forensic medicine. Just as Barnard is recording the article's conclusions, Administrative Judge John Talbert taps a water glass with his spoon to call the meeting to order.

Talbert has risen to the position of administrative judge because of a single talent: he has managed to live forty-eight years without taking a position on any issue, great or small, that could possibly offend anyone. Those who know him are divided into two categories: friends and those who are not his enemies. Barth fits into the latter category since he has not gone out of his way to be Talbert's friend.

Talbert sits at the head of the table, his blue suit still a wrinkleless wonder in early afternoon. Every brown hair on his head is neatly in place. His voice is at perfect pitch for his opening remarks. "I'll be brief because I know that you have busy calendars. In fact, the only remarks I have to make concern those calendars."

He reaches into his inside coat pocket and carefully pulls out a single index card covered with neatly typed numbers. "My statistics for the first quarter of this year show that we, as a group, have disposed of fewer cases than for the same period last year. At the same time, the number of cases coming into our courts has risen 11.3 per cent. Well, we all know what this means. We're falling further and further behind. I'm not sure what we can do about it, because I know we are all working hard. But the fact remains that if something isn't done, it's going to get worse."

"I'm not sure what can be done, John," says Judge David Walker. "But I know this. I can't cope with the calendar I've got now."

Judge Walker's problem would be lessened, Barth reflects, if he would extend his business hours beyond 2:30 P.M. Walker's method has always been the same: he waits until lawyers coming to trial tell him they are prepared to settle the case. Then, he carefully avoids settlement until the remainder of the day's calendar has been postponed in "preparation" for the trial. After this, he calls the attorneys forward and settles their case. With all other items put over for another day, Walker can—and does—go home.

After Walker finishes, Judge George Goodale asks to be heard. "Speaking only for myself," says Goodale, "I don't find the assignments that much of a burden. I've been on the bench for seven years now and don't think that there's ever been a complaint about a delay in my courtroom. Most of the time, I'm calling John Talbert and asking for more cases."

Sure, George, you keep your calendar in order, Barth concedes silently. You do it by getting pleas quickly. And you get pleas quickly because you lean on prosecutors to offer pleas so low that no semiliterate hood can refuse them. You're not really helping the defendants, who go out sneering at the law, knowing they don't get what they deserve. And you don't help the next law-abiding citizen who meets up with your defendant some dark night. But you do make things easier for yourself, with the added attraction that you can brag at these luncheons to the rest of us about your tidy calendar.

"I really do think we have more important things to do than listen to each others' small triumphs and inconveniences," says Tom Cochran wearily. Cochran, in Barth's view, is a man to be listened to with respect. Nobody mistakes Tom Cochran's opinions for those of Holmes or Brandeis. But Cochran is honest, in print as well as in person. He does not pretend to know more than he does. But his quiet, careful approach to the law is disarmingly effective.

"Jails are overflowing," Cochran continues, "and at least for some of us, so are courtroom calendars. Frankly, I'm not certain what I can do differently that will help the situation, but I'm open to suggestions."

"Thanks, Tom," says John Talbert quickly, just as Cochran is about to speak again. "We obviously don't have the time to discuss the problem in any detail today. I just wanted everybody to be aware of the gravity of the situation. My office is, of course, open to all of you at any time. I'll give serious consideration to any suggestions you have. In the meantime, I hope we'll try a little harder to move the calendar along."

"Speaking of moving along," says Talbert, looking at his watch, "I think we'd better get on with our lunch if we're going to be back in our courtrooms by two. If there are no more matters to discuss . . ."

Judge Jack Gordon's hand suddenly shoots up. "I bring this matter up reluctantly," Gordon begins, "but I think it is relevant to our discussion. We are all concerned about crowded calendars. And yet, I must tell you that I find myself on more days than I would like to count waiting for assignments from Judge Barth. I don't know what the problem is, but I do think something ought to be done about it. With all due respect to my colleague, Judge Barth . . ."

"You don't have to give me respect," growls Barth, "because I'll tell you something, Judge Gordon. When it's my turn, I'm not going to return the favor."

There is no next turn. John Talbert coolly declares the meeting adjourned. While Barth and Gordon exchange cold stares, the other judges eat their roast beef.

Soon Barth begins to eat, too; the memory of challenging Jack Gordon lingers in his mind. He knows he shouldn't feel good about his outburst. But he does. Gordon was not raising the issue of assignments because he wanted to seriously discuss the problem. If that were the case, he could easily have brought it up privately. Gordon wanted to do it publicly because, in that way, he would bully Barth the way he does everybody else. Jack Gordon is now on notice that there is somebody around here who will not put up with his bullying. And if Gordon decides it is not a good idea to try to push Jimmy Barth around, he may next come to the conclusion that he should not try to push clerks, court reporters, lawyers, and witnesses around either. If that comes to pass, Judge James Barth ought to receive the mayor's annual public service award. The thought pleases Barth, who finishes his meal without speaking or listening to another word.

2:05 P.M.

"Your Honor," says Barbara Jennings. "I would like to call John Harding as my next witness."

So you've decided to have Mr. Harding testify, Barth is thinking. I think it's a mistake. I can't remember the last time a defendant took the stand and the jury didn't return a guilty verdict. Well, I've been wrong before . . .

John Harding puts his right hand on a Bible, takes the oath, and sits down. He states his name in a deep, assured voice. Then, anticipating Assistant DA Bob Carlin's cross-examination, Barbara moves directly to Harding's criminal record. He has been charged and convicted of gambling, petty larceny and two counts of possession of heroin, he tells the jury. His last arrest for possession of heroin was three years ago.

"Now, Mr. Harding," says Barbara, "let me direct your attention to your activities last June. Were you employed at that time?"

"Yes, ma'am."

"And where were you employed?"

"I worked as a pot washer at the Liberty National Bank cafeteria."

"And that is the cafeteria on the fourteenth floor of the Liberty National Bank Building at 1480 Broad Street. Is that correct?"

"Yes, ma'am."

"How long did you work at the cafeteria, Mr. Harding?"

"Three weeks."

(69)

"Who was your supervisor there?"

"Miss Petersen was on vacation when I was hired. But when she came back, she was my supervisor."

"During those three weeks, did you ever ask Karen Petersen or anyone else for an advance on your salary?"

"No, ma'am."

"Are you certain of that, Mr. Harding?"

"Yes, ma'am."

"Did you ever borrow money for any reason from Miss Petersen?"

"Yes, ma'am."

"When was that?"

"On two occasions, I believe the first and second days that Miss Petersen returned from vacation, I asked to borrow money for cab fare."

"That would have been June eleventh and twelfth?"

"Yes, ma'am."

"And did she give you money?"

"Yes, two dollars each time."

"But you never asked or received an advance on your salary from Miss Petersen?"

"No, ma'am."

"Mr. Harding, when did you quit your job as a pot washer at the cafeteria?"

"My last day of work was Friday, June fifteenth, I think."

"Did you ever return to the cafeteria, for any reason, after June fifteenth."

"No, ma'am."

"Are you sure of that?"

"Yes, ma'am."

"Mr. Harding, can you tell me what you did on the day of June twenty-second?"

"That was my son's birthday. I went to my wife's apartment

and drew some cartoons for my son and watched some plays on TV."

"What time did you go to your wife's apartment on June twenty-second?"

"Some time in the morning, about ten fifteen, I think."

Harding is led through his version of his activities on June twenty-second. His laconic responses to Barbara Jennings's questions support Althea Harding's testimony. He, too, remembers that his son's birthday party began at three o'clock because they were watching "Another World" when the company came. And John Harding knew the party was over at four o'clock because he and Althea began to watch "Somerset" at that time. He left Althea Harding's apartment "about eleven," he says, having spent a pleasant summer day with his wife and son on his son's birthday.

After Barbara finishes her examination, Barth reflects on the defendant's testimony: Harding did all right. Barbara might have played him up a little more. Here is a devoted father spending an entire day with his son on his son's birthday. And she might have said more about his poor, miserable existence. The crack legal aid investigators might have helped, too. Maybe they could have produced little James's birth certificate showing that June 22 was, indeed, his birthday. Or at the very least, found a receipt for a birthday cake to lend some verisimilitude to Mr. and Mrs. Harding's story. Still, if Carlin doesn't do too much damage on cross-examination, Harding's alibi may raise a reasonable doubt of his guilt in at least one juror's mind. And that's all it takes.

Bob Carlin serves notice on Harding that he will be more aggressive in his cross-examination of the defendant than he was with his wife. He directs the jury's attention immediately to Harding's criminal record, suggesting that the defendant's use of heroin was heavy and habitual. The conviction three years ago, Carlin makes the witness admit, had been the result of police finding ninety glassine envelopes of heroin on Harding.

"You were a pusher, weren't you?" asks Carlin.

"No, sir."

"You were caught with ninety glassine envelopes and they were all for you, is that what you're saying?"

"Yes, sir," Harding replies calmly.

"You were convicted of possession of heroin twice, the first time six years ago, and, again, three years ago. Were you using heroin continuously for those years?"

"Yes, sir."

"Were you addicted?"

"No, sir."

"You used heroin for three years continuously and you are testifying under oath that you weren't addicted?"

"Yes, sir."

"Did you commit other crimes to support your habit?"

"Objection," Barbara Jennings says. "The witness has said he was not an addict."

"Sustained," Barth responds.

Carlin thinks he's made his point and moves to Harding's last day on the job at the cafeteria. "Why did you quit your job at the cafeteria, Mr. Harding?"

"I was catching colds coming in and out of the freezer," the defendant answers.

"And you say you quit on June fifteen and didn't return to the cafeteria again?"

"Yes, sir."

"Weren't you owed a check for your last week of work?"

"Yes, sir."

"Why didn't you return to get that check, Mr. Harding?"

"I forgot about it."

"You are saying, Mr. Harding, that though you had no other job or source of income at that time, you didn't collect your last paycheck because you forgot about it."

"Yes, sir."

Carlin pauses a moment to let the jury ponder the defendant's answer.

"Now, Mr. Harding, you heard Miss Petersen testify that you took two twenty dollar advances from her. Was she lying, Mr. Harding?"

"Objection, Your Honor," says Barbara Jennings. "The question is improper on cross-examination."

"Overruled."

"Was Miss Petersen lying, Mr. Harding, when she said she gave you two advances of twenty dollars?"

"Objection."

"Overruled. Answer the question, Mr. Harding," Barth says.

"Yes, sir."

"You heard Miss Petersen and Mrs. Mendoza testify that you were in their office on June twenty-second. Were they lying?"

"Objection," Barbara says.

"Overruled."

"Were they lying, Mr. Harding?"

"Yes, sir."

"Did you ever have any arguments or fights with Miss Petersen or Mrs. Mendoza?"

"No, sir."

"Do you know of any reason why they would want to frame you?"

"No, sir."

"You heard Miss Petersen testify that you cut her throat? Was she lying?"

"Yes, sir."

"And you heard Miss Petersen say you took money from the office safe. Was she lying?"

"Yes sir."

Bob is doing well now, Barth is thinking. He's getting his witness's version of what happened before the jury a second time. And he's forcing the jury to choose between Miss Petersen and Mrs. Mendoza and the defendant as to who's telling the truth. I think this jury will choose Petersen and Mendoza. None of the jurors is very different from Karen Petersen and Sara Mendoza. They aren't all law and order conservatives. But they do care about their own lives, and when they hear of an assault and robbery like this one, they ask: Could this happen to me? The answer is that it could. So they have a stake in seeing that there is some legal order in their community because, without it, they cannot go about their lives as they want to.

It's different for John Harding. It doesn't seem as though anybody, including Harding himself, has given him much care or concern. He's been drifting for years, uneasy with himself and his society. He's casual about his life because he doesn't really value it. He assumes others think the same way. They don't. That's why he's taken a terrible gamble by going to trial before this jury.

Bob Carlin senses that he has a good thing going and methodically leads Harding through the details of Petersen's and Mendoza's testimony, always with the refrain: Were they lying? And each time, John Harding is forced to answer in the affirmative. Relief comes at 5:27 P.M. when Carlin informs Barth that he has no further questions for the defendant.

5:36 P.M.

Two freshly typed legal motions on behalf of defendant Richard Leone, stickup man and model client of Sunshine

House Drug Rehabilitation Center, are on Barth's desk when he returns to his office from court. The first motion, submitted by Leone's lawyer, Henry Simpson, is to dismiss the Leone case on the grounds that since he has already pleaded to one count of possession of drugs in another court he cannot stand trial for armed robbery of the drugstore that provided the drugs. Simpson argues that this would be double jeopardy and prohibited by the Fifth and Fourteenth Amendments of the U.S. Constitution.

As he reads through Simpson's argument, Barth's temper begins to rise. Errant nonsense, he mutters. It's ridiculous to say that if a defendant steals drugs one day and, then, a week later is arrested with the drugs he's stolen, that a conviction on the possession count undercuts the robbery. They're two separate fact situations and two separate crimes. If Henry Simpson was right, the courts would be filled with stickup men rushing to court to plead to a possession count so they couldn't be tried for armed robbery.

Underneath the double jeopardy motion papers, Barth finds the second set of legal papers, demanding that the DA's office produce all of the evidence that it has accumulated in the Leone case. Oh, come on, Henry. The Leone case has been kicking around for almost a year. You've had ample opportunity to ask the DA for and receive whatever evidence that you're entitled to. Just to assure himself that he's right, Barth grabs a copy of the *State Code of Criminal Procedure,* thumbs through it to the section on "pre-trial discovery" and reads: "A motion for discovery by a defendant against whom an indictment is pending must be made with due dilligence prior to the commencement of the trial and if it is not so made it may be summarily denied." Barth underlines the last five words.

Any credibility that Henry Simpson had with me, Barth is thinking, has now evaporated. First, he tries to persuade me that Leone ought to be paroled to Sunshine House. When I don't buy his argument, he runs back to his office and dredges up motions that, even if they had merit, are long overdue. Well, Mr. Simpson is going to be in for a little surprise when he comes in tomorrow morning. I'm going to hit him right between the eyes with his goddamn motions.

Barth looks at his watch. Six o'clock. He's due in half an hour for his law school dinner at the Sheraton. He is slightly amused at his concern to be at the dinner on time. He's practically sworn off formal dinners altogether to avoid the boring speeches and obsequious bowing and scraping from lawyers who appear in his courtroom. His law school class dinner should be different. There, he can share professional childhood memories and swap jokes with friends who remember Jimmy Barth before he was the Honorable Judge Barth. Barth puts on his coat, closes the door to his office, and turns the key.

6:31 P.M.

Two bartenders, in black tux coats and black bow ties, serve Johnny Walker Black Label and J & B on the rocks across the heavy oak bar. The men on the other side puff vigorously on expensive cigars and shout out names of newcomers as they enter.

"Jimmy, Jimmy Barth," calls a heavyset man holding a highball glass.

Barth is pleased with the welcome and looks to the bar for his greeter.

"Over here, Jimmy—excuse me, Judge Barth—over here by the Scotch arsenal."

"That figures," Barth shouts back as he forges his way to the far end of the bar where Bill Tirnauer toasts Barth with a grin and his Scotch on the rocks.

"Bill, how the hell are you?" asks Barth.

"Fine, Jimmy, couldn't be better. And what about His Honor, this evening?" Tirnauer asks with mock humility.

"Terrible," replies Barth. "Cops and robbers is an interesting enough game, but when the robbers outnumber the cops everyday, it ceases to be fun."

"Come on, Jimmy, you love it. You don't have to chase the robbers. All you have to do is sit on your ass in a black robe and look distinguished and speak words of judicial wisdom. It sounds pretty good to me."

"Sure, Bill. Listening to tales of stickup men and rapists and murderers is fun, huh? That's what you call inspiring work? Well, I'll tell you something. Sitting in that fifteenth-floor suite of offices, with the thick carpets, French provincial furniture and hundred-dollar-an-hour clients doesn't sound all that burdensome to me."

"Oh, Jimmy, how you talk," laughs Tirnauer. "Hey, before you get drunk and completely out of hand, I think we'd better go eat." Tirnauer puts his arm on Barth's shoulder and the two slowly walk up the stairs toward the private dining room on the hotel mezzanine. "These dinners are a far cry from Maude's hash and hot coffee we used to live on during exam time," says Tirnauer.

"You're right, Bill. Maude's was better, though I can't say the quality of your conversation was particularly good either then or now," Barth replies drolly.

Tirnauer guffaws.

As they enter the dining room, a short, red-headed man with rimless glasses approaches and asks, "Is Jimmy telling dirty stories again?"

"You only wish," says Barth, as he shakes hands with Martin Sorrels, one of the city's most successful personal injury lawyers.

Barth sits down at one end of the long table and is flanked by Tirnauer and Sorrels, both close law school friends.

Barth eyes the fruit cocktail in front of him and says, "The chef is dazzling us with another example of his incomparable *haute cuisine.*"

"All right, Jimmy," says Sorrels, "we know this is a disappointment to you criminal court judges who try to squeeze in a case now and then between your quiche and pheasant under glass. But we common folks downtown are satisfied."

"*Touché,* Sorrels," says Barth good-naturedly.

As the fruit cocktail is replaced by the French onion soup, Marty Sorrels looks at Barth as if he is about to say something, but remains silent. After taking several spoonfuls of his soup, Sorrels looks at Barth once again and this time speaks. "I've been meaning to ask you something ever since you've been on the bench, Jimmy," he says softly. "I'm just wondering . . . oh, what the hell . . . Jimmy, don't you really think that being a criminal court judge is a little too easy for you?"

Barth looks up from his soup, searching Sorrels's face for a smile or wink, some indication that he's kidding. But there is none. "Marty, are you serious about that question?" Barth asks.

"I am, Jimmy. Don't get me wrong. I'm not trying to put you down. To the contrary. It just seems to me that you're too smart for that job. I remember you in law school. You really dug into the writings of Pound and Edmond Cahn, and when you analyzed a legal problem, you did it layer by layer."

"So what?" asks Barth with a hint of belligerence in his voice.

"I just don't see how you can get the intellectual stimulation you need by taking pleas all day long or presiding over criminal trials. Don't misunderstand me. Somebody has to do it. It's an important job that requires someone with a good brain and sturdy sense of fairness. But not a Jimmy Barth. And I don't mean to say that taking a plea or charging a jury isn't difficult.

(78)

It's just that I think your mind can take in a lot more than that."

By the time that Sorrels has finished, all conversation at Barth's end of the table has stopped and six heads are turned toward him. Barth takes three more spoonfuls of onion soup and carefully wipes his mouth with his napkin. He says nothing but is thinking: Why is it that whenever I go anywhere outside of the courtroom or my apartment, even to a law school class dinner, the conversational pattern is so predictable. Even with good friends like Marty Sorrels and Bill Tirnauer, the jokes and easy banter sooner or later give way to serious talk about my job. It never happened when I was in private practice. But now that I'm a judge, my classmates insist on embarking on an archaeological dig into my professional psyche.

"You don't think being a criminal court judge is stimulating, huh, Marty?" says Barth. "Well, first let me ask you if you think that this magnificent brainpower of mine could be put to better use on the civil side?"

Sorrels nods his head affirmatively.

"And what do you think the intellectual heavyweights on the civil side spend most of their time doing, Marty?"

Sorrels says nothing.

"Well, I'll tell you. They spend most of their time listening to you and your friends argue personal injury cases. Maybe you think that tort law is a greater challenge than criminal law. I don't. For me, the concept of contributory negligence has no greater intrinsic intellectual worth than, say, the issue of what is a reasonable search of a two-bit hood's apartment.

"If it's not the superior intellectual stimulation of a personal injury case, then it must be something else that makes the civil court judge's job more worthwhile. Maybe you think it's the process of working out a settlement. The civil court judge, according to that view, is working profound intellectual wonders by bringing the two sides together on a damage settlement.

"I say that's horseshit. That civil court judge is no more than a glorified purchasing agent, a middleman acting on behalf of the lawyers for the insurance company and of the accident victim. In the end, his settlement does no more than subsidize either the insurance company or the hospital that is billing the victim."

Barth does not invite comment or challenge to his statements. Instead, he continues. "You can be sure that my work does not deliver insights into the nature of justice every Monday through Friday. Sometimes, in fact, I think I am doing nothing grander than running a sputtering shuttle service between courtroom and jail for society's misfits. But every so often, I like to think I'm doing more, that I'm grappling with a jurisprudential problem that has interested philosophers for centuries: How do you maintain a broad, objective rule of law that can be applied fairly to individuals whose backgrounds, motivations, and actual crimes differ radically? Much of the time, it can't be done. Legislatures pass laws that set the limits for my deliberations. I cannot make up the crimes or the punishments. Still, I try to look at the particular circumstances surrounding the criminal act and the individual who is the 'perpetrator.'

"Take two defendants who appeared in my courtroom today. The first was a hood with a long record who stuck up a drugstore and, given the chance, will do it again. The second was a twenty-four-year-old defendant on trial for assaulting his boss with a knife and sacking the office safe. I think the second defendant was acting on an angry impulse. I know it was his first arrest for a serious crime. There is a difference in those two crimes, just as I think there is a difference between the veteran stickup man who is a constant danger to society and the defendant with no serious record who is not. Frequently, these weighty considerations are reduced to whether I can get a DA to come down a few years in the plea he'll offer a young defendant, or make a defense attorney talk turkey to a seasoned hood. But there's substance, I think, behind these endless, often frustrating, plea-bargaining sessions and criminal trials. When an individual's liberty is at issue, the stakes are high. And what may appear to you, Marty, as an exercise in futility, is to me very serious professional business."

Barth suddenly realizes that he has monopolized the conversation at his end of the table. His eyes move from Marty Sorrels to Bill Tirnauer to the four other classmates who have given him rapt attention. He did not mean to turn the dinner conversation into a monologue. But that's what has happened. His filet mignon is lukewarm and untouched. Everybody knows that Marty Sorrels has pricked one of Barth's sensitive nerves and Jimmy Barth has let out a brief but agonized scream. That isn't supposed to happen at law school dinners.

Barth's classmates struggle through limp discussions of the new state no-fault law, the National Basketball Association's playoffs, and the outrageously high price that a good bottle of Bordeaux now commands. But it's no use. Neither humor nor information is really exchanged. The evening is lost, as far as Barth is concerned, and it's his fault. Why couldn't he have just brushed off Marty Sorrels's question with a fast quip and gotten on with a light-hearted evening? Too late now. When the chocolate mousse is served, Barth complains of a headache, quietly excuses himself, and leaves the dinner party.

III
Wednesday

9:25 A.M.

Henry Simpson has selected his freshly pressed three-piece brown herringbone suit to wear today, the one that he usually reserves for family weddings, testimonial dinners, and summations to juries. Today, Henry has no wedding or testimonial dinner or jury summation scheduled but he is wearing his best suit, nonetheless. The reason is that Henry Simpson anticipates a special appearance before Judge Barth. His best suit will help, Henry thinks, though he knows that his arguments on behalf of his client, Richard Leone, must also be first class.

As he sits in the first row of seats in Courtroom 27, next to Leone, Henry takes one last look at an index card with notes on the Leone case (charge: armed robbery of the Park Hill Drug Store, July 3, 1973 . . .). Then, he looks up at the empty bench and imagines the next courtroom scene as he hopes that it will unfold: First, Judge Barth will call Henry forward and commend him for the superior draftsmanship of the two legal motions that he sent Barth yesterday afternoon. Barth will ask

Simpson for additional legal authority for his motion to dismiss the case on the ground that Leone will be placed in double jeopardy if he goes to trial on the armed robbery charge, since he has already taken a plea for possession of drugs. Simpson will respond by submitting a carefully honed list of five legal precedents for his motion to dismiss, complete with citations. He will hestiate slightly after announcing each citation, subtly suggesting to Barth that he has not lifted them from a single judicial opinion but, rather, has read each case, digested it, and is prepared (though not anxious) to argue both the facts and law of the matter. Barth will realize that Simpson knows his law, concede his legal point, and grant the motion to dismiss the case. Simpson will thank the judge, not effusively, mind you, but with the dignity judges have come to expect from Henry Simpson, Esq., and then he will walk back to the counsel table to accept the gratitude and congratulations of his client, Richard Leone.

Simpson snaps out of his reverie as the bulky figure of Judge James Barth emerges at the bench. Barth unceremoniously plops down in his chair and says a few words to George Giles. With a rough, sweeping motion of his right arm, he waves Simpson forward. Simpson deposits his client, Leone, at the defense table, then marches smartly to the bench. But when Simpson reaches the bench, Barth points Henry back to the defense table.

"Call the Leone case, George," growls Barth.

"Case number one on the calendar, Richard Leone," Giles announces.

"Mr. Simpson," says Barth, looking directly at Henry, "you have submitted two motions on behalf of your client, Richard Leone. The first is a motion for a bill of particulars of all evidence in the district attorney's possession. The second is a motion to dismiss the case on the grounds that the defendant will stand in double jeopardy if he is tried on the armed robbery charge since he has already pleaded guilty to possession of drugs. Both motions are denied."

The word "denied" has no visible effect on Richard Leone, who does not change his vacant expression. Simpson retains his serious demeanor and, at the same time, reaches into his right coat pocket for the index card on which he has typed his notes.

Speaking in a gruff but formal manner, Barth continues: "Mr. Simpson, your motion for a bill of particulars is long overdue. The Leone case has been on the docket for almost a year. You have had ample time to request and receive all of the evidence that is coming to you from the district attorney's office. I am not obligated at this late hour to grant your motion. I refer you to Section 799 of the State Code of Criminal Procedure for authority for my decision to deny your motion.

"Your second motion is also denied because your claim that Mr. Leone has been placed in double jeopardy is without merit. The two charges, possession of drugs and armed robbery in the first degree, are separate crimes. Mr. Leone may, as he did, plead guilty to the charge of possession of drugs in one court and still face charges of armed robbery. His plea on the first charge does not release him from responsibility in the second. That takes care of your motions, Mr. Simpson. The case is ready for trial."

"Your Honor," says Simpson. "I request an opportunity for oral argument of the motions."

"The request is denied," snaps Barth. "Anything else?"

"May I approach the bench?" asks Simpson.

"No, you may not. This case is ready for trial. You'll begin jury selection next Monday."

"Your Honor, I would again ask that I may be allowed to approach the bench," pleads Simpson.

"Mr. Simpson, you are delaying my calendar. Mr. Giles, call in the Harding jury."

Henry Simpson's right hand, which has remained in his coat

pocket throughout his dialogue with Barth, crumples the index card that he had readied for his anticipated oral argument on the motions. He searches for a word, a phrase, a sentence that will miraculously reopen the discussion with Barth. But nothing comes to mind as Giles leaves his desk to bring in the Harding jury. Barth's head is down now, ignoring Henry Simpson, who remains at the counsel table. Simpson is tapped gently on the shoulder by Court Officer Alfred Lorenzo and asked to leave. Simpson shrugs his shoulders, takes Leone by the arm, and slowly walks out of the courtroom.

Outside Courtroom 27, Barbara Jennings is being told by her superior at legal aid, Jerry Chester, that she should present her summation to the Harding jury in a calm, rational manner. Chester, speaking and gesturing with staccato quickness, has been giving the same pep talk to young attorneys for the twenty years that he has been a legal aid supervisor.

"Look, Barbara," says Chester in a tough but sympathetic voice, "this jury hasn't put in the time on this case that you have. You know the facts better than they do. And you know the law. Just give it to them straight. No frills. No tricks. Just straight. I know you can do it." He pats her on the shoulder before heading for another courtroom with another legal aid attorney in distress.

Barbara watches Chester for a moment, then turns and pushes open the door to Courtroom 27. Her client, John Harding, is already seated at the defense table and Assistant District Attorney Bob Carlin is across the aisle at the prosecutor's table. Barbara walks down the center aisle, pretending casualness and confidence. She hopes that the powder she has dabbed under her eyes will hide the circles that have formed after three hours sleep. Most of the night had been spent preparing her summation, not only typing an outline (I. Issues of reasonable doubt; II. Events according to prosecution witnesses; III. Attack on prosecution witnesses' testimony) but practicing her presentation over and over again before the bathroom mirror.

Barbara nods to her client, Harding, and to Bob Carlin. She tries to make small talk, the kind that she supposes the best trial lawyers engage in before their summations. A comment on the rainy morning, on Bob Carlin's red and white polka dot bow tie and then . . .

"The People versus John Harding," announces George Giles. "Is the defense ready to proceed?" he asks.

"Yes," says Barbara.

"Are the People ready to proceed?"

"Yes," says Bob.

"Your Honor, the jury is present and accounted for. Both defense and prosecution are ready to proceed," reports Giles.

"Miss Jennings," says Barth, "you may begin your summation."

Barbara Jennings takes one last anxious glance at her client, John Harding, and walks to the railing to face the twelve jurors. Her right hand shakes slightly as she places a yellow legal pad with her outline on it on the railing. She waits until she has steadied her legal pad and fully composed herself before she looks directly at the jurors. She speaks in a soft, tentative voice:

"Ladies and gentlemen, the law requires that if you have any reasonable doubt about the guilt of John Harding, you must find him not guilty. I am going to suggest to you this morning that many reasonable doubts have been raised about the defendant's guilt throughout the trial.

"Picture the events as Miss Petersen and Mrs. Mendoza remembered them. A man entered their Liberty National Bank cafeteria office on June twenty-second without their realizing it. By their own accounts, he was in the office less than fifteen minutes. For at least ten minutes, both women were tied up and placed face down on the floor. They could not see the man for those ten minutes. For the remaining time, the man terrorized the two women. He shouted at them and threatened them. It was an extremely traumatic experience for Miss Petersen and Mrs. Mendoza. Given the pressure and stress of that experience, wouldn't you forget some important details? I think they did."

As Barbara Jennings begins to gain confidence, her questions become more challenging and her voice more assertive. "Isn't it possible that Miss Petersen assumed that her attacker must have been the defendant because he was the last person to quit his job? I submit to you that this is what happened. A psychological transference occurred. I suggest that Karen Petersen and Mrs. Mendoza discussed the attack and convinced themselves that the attacker was John Harding. Whether John Harding actually was the attacker is another question.

"If Miss Petersen were certain that her attacker was John Harding, why couldn't she give a clear description of him? She didn't say how tall he was or what color shirt he was wearing or even what his face looked like. No, all that Miss Petersen told you and told the police was that it was John Harding. Doesn't that alone create a reasonable doubt in your minds?"

The young attorney puts her hands into her suit pocket and begins to pace about, looking up at the courtroom walls rather than at the jury. "John Harding was not required to take the witness stand. But he did. And John Harding told you that he was not at the bank cafeteria on June twenty-second. He told you he was at his wife's apartment all day. And his wife, Althea Harding, told you the same thing. Doesn't it make sense that on June twenty-second, the birthday of the Hardings' son, that Mr. and Mrs. Harding would want to be with their son? Don't all of us want to be with our loved ones on their birthdays?

"Althea Harding, John Harding's wife, told you that her husband was with her and their two-year-old son, James, all day on June twenty-second. It was not easy for Mrs. Harding to testify and be subjected to the rigorous cross-examination of the district attorney. I ask that you consider Mrs. Harding's testimony carefully. She knows there could be dire consequences for her if she lied under oath.

"The judge may tell you in his instructions that John Harding and his wife are interested witnesses. Certainly, they are interested in the outcome of the case. I don't deny it. But because they are interested in the outcome is no reason for them not to testify. Remember, John Harding and his wife don't have to prove that the defendant was in his wife's apartment at three fifteen on the afternoon of June twenty-second. The burden is on the district attorney to prove he was not. And he must prove that to you, ladies and gentlemen, beyond a reasonable doubt.

"I am asking you to use your common sense. Is it reasonable to think that the defendant would have acted in the manner that has been described by the district attorney? Does it make sense that John Harding, if he had planned this assault and robbery, would have been so conspicuous about it? Wouldn't the person who did this want to be as inconspicuous as possible?

"If he were planning a robbery, would John Harding have borrowed money from the person he was going to rob? If John Harding had planned the robbery of his own employer, wouldn't he at least have worn a mask so that his employers wouldn't recognize him? And if John Harding had committed this robbery, wouldn't he have run away instead of staying in his apartment until his arrest? Is this the behavior of someone who has committed an assault and robbery? I don't think so."

Barbara pauses to let her arguments sink in. "I am sure,"

says an unsure Barbara Jennings, "you won't convict John Harding because his life-style may seem unstructured, compared to your own. John Harding's life-style is not an issue here, ladies and gentlemen. And I am sure you won't convict John Harding because he has an irregular work history or because he has a criminal record." Barbara Jennings surveys the jury, searching for a smile, a nod, any sign that the jurors understand and accept her point. But there is none.

She nervously clears her throat, then continues. "As I said before, I am not suggesting that Karen Petersen lied to you. I am suggesting that she mistakenly identified the defendant. Miss Petersen underwent a very traumatic experience. Is it not reasonable to expect her to forget some of the details of that experience, given the pressure and stress of the experience? And isn't it more reasonable to believe John Harding's story that he borrowed two dollars for cab fare rather than Miss Petersen's, that he asked for a forty dollar advance the very week that he met her? I ask you, ladies and gentlemen, which story is more believable?

"I am not going to review all of the testimony in this trial. It is probably still fresh in your minds. You might ask, why didn't Diane Smith, Mrs. Harding's sister, testify since she was at the birthday party on June twenty-second at Althea Harding's apartment? But I want to remind you again, the defense has no burden to prove John Harding's *innocence* beyond a reasonable doubt. You must decide if the district attorney has proved his *guilt* beyond a reasonable doubt.

"I submit that the district attorney's version of the crime just doesn't make sense. The improbability of it all is enough to raise a reasonable doubt. And I suggest that John Harding's and Althea Harding's testimony, their testimony alone, is sufficient to raise a reasonable doubt of the defendant's guilt. You must remember, you cannot convict my client even if you think he is *probably* guilty. The district attorney must prove his guilt beyond a reasonable doubt. He has not done it."

Barbara Jennings pauses to scan her notes. Satisfied that she has covered all of the points in her outline, she says, "Thank you for your attention," grabs her legal pad from the railing, and walks quickly back to the defense table. After she sits down, she allows herself a tight little smile of relief.

Bob Carlin springs to his feet at Barth's signal. He studies the jurors and then speaks in a strong, confident voice. "Today, ladies and gentlemen of the jury, I want to appeal to your common sense. The issue is simple in this case. Did the defendant, John Harding, force his way into the office of Karen Petersen on June twenty-second, take twenty-four hundred dollars from the office safe, cut Karen Petersen's throat, and run away? I don't think there can be any doubt that John Harding did all of these things. The evidence is overwhelming.

"Since there really is no doubt that John Harding committed these crimes, you might ask, *why* did he commit them? The defendant's behavior was irrational. We all can agree on that. But all crime is irrational. You and I aren't psychologists. We aren't trained in psychoanalysis. Why John Harding acted as he did is not your concern. What his sentence should be, as the judge will tell you, is not your concern either. You are here to determine the facts in the case. You are here to weigh the evidence and decide what actually happened. What are the facts? The defendant, John Harding, forcibly entered the business office of the cafeteria on the fourteenth floor of the Liberty National Bank Building at about three fifteen P.M. on June twenty-second."

Until this point, Bob has delivered his summation with a steady cadence. But when he speaks of John Harding "sneaking up" behind Karen Petersen, putting his arm around her neck, and, later, slitting her throat, the DA's face tightens, his voice becomes shrill. And when he recalls Sara Mendoza's pleading with the defendant—"John, John. Think of your mother, think of your father"—Bob Carlin is all sorrow and soul.

"I didn't make up this story. You heard it from Miss Karen Petersen and Mrs. Sara Mendoza, both intelligent, credible witnesses. They told you the truth. Karen Petersen is the supervisor of a large cafeteria staff. She is a responsible citizen. She has no reason to lie. And Mrs. Mendoza? That woman is pure truth. Pure truth." Carlin pauses for effect. "Miss Petersen, Mrs. Mendoza, and John Harding worked in the same cafeteria. It is just impossible that these two intelligent, responsible women could make a mistake in identifying John Harding and telling you about his violent, criminal acts.

"Miss Jennings can't say anything in her client's defense and doesn't. The only thing she can do is let John Harding and his wife take the witness stand and lie. How can anyone believe their so-called alibi defense? They are lying. John Harding wants to get off and his wife wants him back. That's why they lied. Where is the sister who was at that so-called birthday party? If John Harding's alibi were true, you can be sure she would have been here.

"Miss Jennings has been nit-picking because she has no case. She talks about the identification of John Harding. We have the best identification possible. The victims *knew* John Harding before the crime. That's very unusual. Miss Jennings says that Karen Petersen couldn't remember what John Harding wore when he assaulted her. Well, I can't tell you exactly what Miss Jennings wore Monday but I know she was here.

"I told you during my opening statement that the People had the obligation to prove the defendant's guilt on all charges beyond a reasonable doubt. I suggest that we can go one step

(94)

further. I suggest that we have proven John Harding's guilt beyond *any* doubt. That's not because I'm a legal genius. I'm not. But this is an airtight case. John Harding is guilty as charged of assaulting Karen Petersen and slitting her throat with a knife, and of taking twenty-four hundred dollars from the cafeteria office safe."

Carlin paces back and forth before the jury three times, head down, appearing deep in thought. He stops suddenly. "Your job isn't an easy one. It is not easy to send someone to prison. But you are here to do your duty. As good citizens, you must do your duty. And that duty," says Carlin, raising his left arm and pointing at the defendant, "is to find John Harding guilty on all charges."

11:19 A.M.

During the midmorning recess of the Harding trial, Melvin Rich, Barth's assistant, marches double-time to the bench.

"Judge," Rich whispers loudly to Barth, "Judge Gordon says he has no cases."

"Judge Gordon has got seventeen cases," Barth replies curtly. "I'm not giving him anything else until he's down to four or five. Judge Gordon thinks that he can ask for and receive cases as he pleases. But that's not going to happen. The fact that he has seventeen cases is enough for me. I have no intention of giving him any more until he has disposed of the cases he has. Tell him that."

Melvin's profound uneasiness at being caught in the middle of a fight between two judges shows in his furrowed brow and nervous twitching.

"Judge," he says, "you know Gordon has had a problem with his case on trial. The prosecution's chief witness has disappeared . . ."

"I know that," Barth cuts in. "But he still has sixteen other cases to work on. Now you go tell him to do it."

Melvin, who knows that he has been summarily dismissed, does an about face and marches out of the courtroom.

Barth is boiling. *Jack Gordon is not going to push me around. I've given him plenty to do. He has complete control of those seventeen cases that I assigned him. If the lawyers try to screw around, it's up to him to get them moving, either toward a plea or a trial.*

Barth realizes that his annoyance with Judge Gordon has momentarily delayed the progress of the Harding trial. He snaps out of his angry mood and is about to tell Giles to bring in the Harding jury, when Judge Jack Gordon, black robes billowing, enters the courtroom and strides to the bench.

"I have no cases," Gordon says indignantly.

"Whadaya mean?" snarls Barth. "You've got seventeen cases."

"You show me," says Gordon evenly, struggling to control his temper. "I'm telling you, I don't have anything ready."

Court officers and attorneys have now gathered for the spectacle of two judges arguing in open court. Barth is unconcerned.

"I just sent you a case yesterday," he growls.

"But the prosecution isn't ready," says Gordon. Suddenly, he looks around and notices his audience. "Could I speak to you in chambers?" he asks. "This isn't a matter I want to discuss in open court."

"No," says Barth. "I'm in the middle of a trial."

"Then do you have a few minutes before lunch?" Gordon asks.

"No, I don't," says Barth. "If I speak to you, it'll spoil my lunch."

Gordon's only reaction to Barth's squelch is to stare for a few brief moments at his tormentor and then to walk out of the courtroom as he walked in, shoulders erect, robes billowing.

After the Harding jury has returned, George Giles announces to Mrs. Murphy and three other regulars that Barth is about to charge the jury and that no one will be permitted to enter or leave the courtroom during the charge. Mrs. Murphy stays for the penultimate scene in her featured drama of the day. The others leave.

Barth arranges his notes in front of him and places a copy of the *State Penal Code* on one side for easy reference. Unlike many of his colleagues, Barth avoids anecdotes or colorful quotations to illustrate a legal point in his charge, fearing that the point might be misinterpreted by a juror. His instructions are, by design, brief and direct.

At the outset, Barth tells the jury that the charges in the indictment against John Harding are accusations and are not to be considered evidence. The prosecutor has the burden of overcoming the defendant's presumption of innocence and that burden of proof never shifts. A defendant can only be convicted if the jury believes his guilt beyond a reasonable doubt. Barth defines reasonable doubt "as an honest doubt which prevents a juror from saying that the defendant is guilty."

The jurors alone, Barth says, must be the sole judges of a witness's credibility. "Miss Jennings and Mr. Carlin have, in their summations, tried to persuade you of what the witnesses have testified to and to how much weight you should give each witness's testimony. You ladies and gentlemen may accept or reject their views as you think the evidence warrants."

Barth then gives the jury the sparest of guidelines for evaluating the credibility of the prosecution's witnesses: "A policeman's testimony," he says, "should not be given more or less weight because of his position as a police officer. Identification testimony by any witness should be received with caution and scrutinized with care. There is always room for human error."

Without mentioning John or Althea Harding by name, Barth suggests to the jury dos and don'ts for evaluating their testimony: "The fact that a witness has a prior criminal record may be considered by the jury in its evaluation of a witness's credibility but," Barth warns, "that record should have no influence in the jury's evaluation of the present charges. A defendant is always an interested witness," says Barth, "but that is only one factor for you to weigh. If you think a witness is truthful, you are not required to disbelieve the testimony because it is given by an interested witness.

"Alibi is a Latin word meaning elsewhere. If true, an alibi is the strongest evidence of innocence. If you believe an alibi or if that alibi creates a reasonable doubt in your mind as to the guilt of the defendant, you must vote for an acquittal. Even if you don't believe an alibi, that is only one factor in weighing a defendant's guilt or innocence."

Barth now pushes aside his notes, places the volume of the *State Penal Code* directly in front of him and opens it to the first of four marked pages. "The first count of the indictment," he says, "is grand larceny in the second degree. To find the defendant, John Harding, guilty of grand larceny in the second degree, you must find that he stole property valued in excess of fifteen hundred dollars." As he always does in his instructions, Barth then reads the definition of legal terms verbatim from the penal code ("Property means any money, personal property . . .").

"The second count of the indictment is robbery in the first degree. To find John Harding guilty of this charge, you must conclude that the defendant forcibly stole a sum of money and, in the course of the commission of the crime, he used or threatened the use of a dangerous instrument.

(98)

"The third count of the indictment charges the defendant with the possession of a dangerous weapon or instrument. To find the defendant guilty of this charge, you must conclude that John Harding possessed a dangerous weapon or instrument with the intention to use that weapon or object unlawfully to harm others.

"The last count of the indictment is the charge of assault in the second degree. To be found guilty of the charge, John Harding must have intended to cause physical injury to Karen Petersen in the course of a felony and have caused such injury to Miss Petersen."

Barth closes his copy of the *State Penal Code* and surveys the faces of the jurors. For the first time during his instructions, he smiles. "Ladies and gentlemen," he says amiably, "there is no formula for evaluating the evidence. You don't have the advantages of television's instant replay and stop action. Listen to the views of your fellow jurors. And use your common sense."

Barth glances at the courtroom clock and then again addresses the jury: "It is twelve fifteen. The court officers have ordered lunch for you. It should be in your conference room by now. The table is small. I would suggest that you finish your lunch and clear away your dishes before you begin deliberations. If you have any further questions, you should communicate them to me in writing through the court officer who will be waiting outside the conference room."

Court Officer Alfred Lorenzo silently walks to the railing and stands, like an honor guard, while the jurors pass, led by fellow Court Officer Sam Mitchell. The jurors are serious, but not solemn. A few, including a wispy little man who used to sell vacuum cleaners, smile at Barth as they pass the bench, then again assume their serious demeanor as they leave the courtroom.

While Barth is still at the bench taking care of paper-work, an unhappy Barbara Jennings, who had left the court-room after Barth had dismissed the jury, returns. She is accompanied by her boss, Jerry Chester. Chester dispenses with the easy banter that usually serves as the prologue to serious conversations between him and Barth.

"Judge, I want you to order Barbara Jennings to remain in this courtroom while the jury is out," Chester demands.

Nobody tells Jimmy Barth how to handle his job. Someone who enjoys less credibility and goodwill with him than Chester would be cut short right there. But he and Chester go back a few years and Barth is willing to listen. His only response to Chester's ultimatum is a cocked eyebrow.

"Judge Gordon has ordered Miss Jennings to begin another trial in his courtroom immediately. I've tried to plead with him on her behalf but he won't listen."

"I can't tell Judge Gordon how to run his courtroom," says Barth. "I don't think it's necessary that Miss Jennings be here while the jury is out. The only thing she is obliged to do is poll the jury if it comes in with a guilty verdict. I don't think that is too great a burden."

Chester's eyes narrow, his voice drops down an octave for dramatic effect. "Judge, legal aid attorneys can't be bounced around like tennis balls. Barbara needs time to rest and reflect on this Harding case. She can't start another one right away." There is a subtle hint of good humor mixed with Chester's anger. He is saying, in effect, "Look, Judge, we both know Jack Gordon is a jackass. Don't let him lean on Barbara. It's not that she really has to be here, but damn it, she doesn't really have to be in Gordon's court either. He can wait a day and let her recover from a rough trial experience."

But Barth refuses to bend. "Another trial will be good for Miss Jennings. It's the best training a young lawyer can get," he says in a friendly but conclusive manner.

"But, Judge," Chester protests, "no lawyer ought to have trials back to back. Barbara's not prepared for this other trial. You wouldn't want to give back-to-back instructions to two different juries, would you?"

"It wouldn't bother me a bit," Barth retorts, "if I had prepared well."

"Well, you know you'd rather not, even if you had prepared well. Barbara has gone through a tough trial; she just isn't ready for another right away. I'm asking you to order her to stay in your courtroom."

"I can't do that. I can't control Judge Gordon's calendar," Barth says. He is thinking, however, that he could do what Chester requests, but it would be bad judicial politics. Gordon is a big enough pain in the ass as it is. I'm not giving him any excuse to make it harder on me. If I keep Barbara here, Jack Gordon can go over my head and complain that I'm meddling in his business. And he would have a point. My only control over him, as an assignment judge, is to send him cases. Once I've done that, I can't interfere.

Chester persists. "Sure, you can keep Barbara here. You're a criminal court judge. You can do anything you want to. Look at Barbara. She's exhausted. Aren't you, Barbara?"

"I am pretty tired," she says reluctantly.

"She looks wonderful to me," Barth says. He'd like Barbara's and Jerry's goodwill but not at the price of more aggravation from Jack Gordon. "Have the DA take a long time with the jury selection, then you can rest there."

"I guess I'm losing ground," Chester says, smiling now.

"I'm telling you, Barbara has no problem," Barth says reassuringly. "She conducted this case well and I'm sure she'll do the same in Judge Gordon's courtroom. Now go show Judge

Gordon your stuff, Barbara," says Barth as he rises and waves to Barbara Jennings and Jerry Chester on his way out of the courtroom.

"Any calls, Betsy?" Barth asks as he enters his office.

"Judge Talbert. He wants you to call him."

Barth sits down at his desk, picks up the telephone, and calls Talbert's number.

"This is Judge Barth. Is Judge Talbert there?" A moment later Talbert's voice is heard at the other end of the phone.

"Yes, John. Sure," Barth responds. "I've got a jury out in the Harding case but that's no problem. Send them in after lunch. Don't mention it. Good-bye."

"Betsy," Barth says, "call George Giles and tell him we've got another trial scheduled for this afternoon. Tell him to have everybody ready by two. And, Betsy, I'm not taking any more calls."

Barth shuts the door to his office, switches on the cassette recording of Bob Dylan's "Blowin' in the Wind," and sits down to a club sandwich and a diet Pepsi that Betsy has ordered from a nearby sandwich shop. Melvin Rich has placed a folder with the label ROGER GILBERT on the outside next to Barth's napkin. This will be a working lunch.

The Roger Gilbert case began with one of the slickest robberies in the city's history: At precisely 3:05 P.M. on February 2, 1973, an immaculately groomed and handsomely dressed man knocked at the basement entrance to the safe deposit department of the First National Bank. The security guard on duty motioned to the man to come back the next day. It was closing time. But the customer persisted. There were important papers in his safe deposit box which he must have that afternoon to close a business deal, he said. The guard hesitated. The customer pleaded. Finally, after the man had shown what the guard thought was proper identification, the guard opened the steel cage door.

To the guard's astonishment, the man quickly put a pistol to his ribs. A second man slipped in and pushed the guard out of sight of passers-by. Then he quickly handcuffed the guard, tied his legs with nylon rope, and attached strips of adhesive tape to his eyes and mouth.

While the second man stood watch, his partner proceeded to the vault room where he pulled out a penciled diagram of the wall of safe deposit boxes.When he came to the boxes which the diagram indicated were filled with the jewelry of the bank's wealthiest customers, he paused. Each of the safe deposit boxes was secured by a door one-half inch thick. The man ignored the doors and simply separated the hinges from the doors with the help of a small hammer and chisel. Within fifteen minutes, he had cleaned out twenty-two safe deposit boxes. At 3:30, the thief calmly put more than two million dollars' worth of jewelry into his oversized attaché case and, with his accomplice, walked out the same basement door they had entered twenty-five minutes earlier.

Thanks to an FBI informer's tip, the safe deposit box looter was identified as Roger Gilbert. Police caught up with Gilbert only six days after the robbery. They searched his quarters and found more than half the jewelry taken from the safe deposit boxes. The city's newspapers lauded the work of the police department, and the police, whose media image had been suffering, happily took their bows.

But Jimmy Rollins, the assistant district attorney assigned to prosecute the case, was not so happy with the turn of events. The cops could make their arrests and forget about the case. But Rollins had to build his prosecution carefully and within the confines of the law's technicalities. He was immediately confronted with a serious problem involving the sensitive diplomatic relations between the city police and the FBI.

Though the city police and the FBI had worked together on the robbery, the cooperation had been, at best, uneasy. After the FBI informer broke the case, that fragile cooperation shattered altogether. The FBI said that it would not make its informer available at the trial because he was too valuable to the Bureau in other pending investigations.

The FBI's refusal to cooperate would, Rollins knew, pose a critical obstacle at Roger Gilbert's pre-trial hearing. Undoubtedly, Gilbert's attorney would say that the cops had no reason to search Gilbert's apartment and that unreasonable searches were a violation of the Fourth and Fourteenth Amendments of the U.S. Constitution. If the judge accepted that argument, and there was a good chance that he would if the FBI informer did not testify as to the basis of the tip, the recovered jewelry could not be used as evidence at the trial. That alone could seriously jeopardize Rollins's prosecution of Gilbert.

Judge Randolph Pearson, who was assigned the Gilbert case, never ruled on the pre-trial defense motion to suppress the jewelry from evidence. According to the official court record, he didn't have to, because Roger Gilbert pleaded guilty to *attempted* armed robbery before attorneys completed their pre-trial suppression arguments. Pearson later sentenced Gilbert to fifteen years in the state penitentiary for his crime. A tidy disposition for a sticky case. Except for one problem: When Judge Pearson announced the fifteen-year sentence in open court, Roger Gilbert jumped out of his chair and shouted "Double-cross." Assistant District Attorney Jimmy Rollins and Gilbert's own attorney, Whitney Barnes, stepped aside as the defendant rushed to the bench and confronted the judge. "You were the one who talked me into this deal, Judge," Gilbert yelled. "I didn't want to take this plea. But you kept saying, 'Trust me, trust me.' So I trusted you and now you've double-crossed me. We agreed on a top of five last summer and you know it. So does my attorney. You're not going to get away with it, Judge. I'm going to fight you. You said I would do no more than five years state time, and we're going to make it stick."

(104)

Judge Pearson, whose capacity for unflappability was sorely taxed that morning, simply stared at Roger Gilbert and said nothing. Finally, the judge responded with a quiet, perfunctory denial of Gilbert's charge. He had not, he said, promised a maximum of five years in prison to the defendant and the fifteen-year sentence was both proper and, now, legally binding.

That might have been the end of the matter except for the actions of two men, Roger Gilbert and his attorney, Whitney Barnes. During his long career as a jewel thief (and defendant), Gilbert had become a devoted student of the law. His study strongly suggested to Gilbert that Judge Pearson's "double-cross" violated every notion of fairness that he had heard expressed in his many court appearances. From prison, Gilbert filed a motion to set aside the judge's sentence on the grounds that Pearson had not lived up to his side of the off-the-record plea agreement. Whitney Barnes filed an affidavit supporting his client's charge that Judge Pearson had manipulated and, ultimately, deceived Roger Gilbert.

Only rarely will a defendant openly challenge the integrity of a sitting judge. Rarer still will an attorney join in the accusation. Barth had been given the sensitive judicial task of deciding who was telling the truth, Judge Pearson or veteran jewel thief Roger Gilbert and his attorney.

Why did Administrative Judge John Talbert assign the case to me? asks Barth as he stares at the Gilbert folder. The first theory that Barth poses in his own mind is that Talbert had decided that James Barth was the only judge on the bench with the requisite competence, integrity, and guts to get to the bottom of such a serious charge against a fellow jurist. Yes, thinks Barth, and tomorrow I will be the newly crowned Choygal of Sikkim.

Barth finds his second theory more believable. Although John Talbert is new in his administrative position, he is well aware that more than one of Barth's colleagues would be delighted to see him fall flat on his face. Barth is not a member of that inner social circle of judges that makes up "the club." What is worse, in the eyes of club members, Barth doesn't aspire to join them. Instead of socializing with his colleagues, Barth had decided several years ago that he preferred to spend extra time on his cases or reading a new political biography or taking Helen to the opera. In handing Barth the Gilbert case, John Talbert might have calculated that he could make some more friends.

Barth considers the most obvious dispositions of the Gilbert case and their consequences. If I conclude that Judge Pearson was not a party to any deception, I will please Pearson and evoke howls of laughter from many of my colleagues. Here is Jimmy Barth, they'll say, so irascible, so anxious to knock us. But when the chips are down, he's no different from the rest of us. He'll protect his own because he knows he may need that same consideration some day. Barth cringes at the thought.

If I find Judge Pearson guilty as charged by Roger Gilbert, that will mean taking a jewel thief's word against that of a state criminal court judge. And my colleagues will say I bullied a fellow judge because I'm such a vindictive SOB. Barth shifts uncomfortably in his chair. I'd better be careful to play this one down the middle, he warns himself. John Talbert may think I'm going to fall on my face, but I've got news for him. I'm not going to do it.

Barth begins his study of the Gilbert case by taking out the transcript of the hearing held in his courtroom last week in which Gilbert and his attorney, Whitney Barnes, had reiterated their charge that Judge Randolph Pearson promised Gilbert a five-year sentence and then gave him fifteen. According to Barnes's testimony, the setup had begun weeks before Gilbert's plea when Judge Pearson had speculated on how he might rule on the defense motion to suppress from evidence at the trial the jewelry found in Gilbert's apartment. The ruling,

(106)

all knew, might have been critical to the ultimate outcome of the trial.

Attorney Barnes had testified: "Judge Pearson had been skillfully playing off the district attorney against me, letting the district attorney believe that he was going to deny the motion, then telling me that he was going to grant the motion. And reversing back and forth. Then he ordered us to begin jury selection. When I asked the judge to rule on the pre-trial motion, he just smiled and wouldn't commit himself. Then he told us to begin selecting a jury."

"Did you object to selecting a jury before Judge Pearson had ruled on the suppression motion?" Barnes had been asked by Carl Elliot, Roger Gilbert's attorney for the hearing (since Barnes was a key witness).

"I certainly did," Barnes had testified. "I told him that his ruling would affect my strategy for selecting a jury. I also told him I thought that selecting a jury before receiving a ruling on the suppression motion was a violation of the State Code of Criminal Procedure."

"And what did Judge Pearson say?" Barnes had been asked.

"He didn't say anything except to order us to begin jury selection," Barnes had replied.

"When did the plea-bargaining sessions with Judge Pearson begin?"

"Well, after two weeks or so of hearing arguments on the suppression motion in the morning and selecting a jury in the afternoon, Judge Pearson called us in and suggested to us that it was the appropriate time to reach a plea bargain. Then we went to lunch and the judge played host. He wouldn't allow anybody to pick up the check and we had a very amiable lunch, and during the course of the lunch, Judge Pearson again strongly suggested that the case could be disposed of. Despite these plea-bargaining sessions with Judge Pearson, the district attorney and I remained far apart. Then, one day Judge Pearson called me into his robing room. He told me that if Gilbert would plead guilty to attempted robbery, I had his assurance that Gilbert would receive a sentence of no more than five years. 'I can give him as little as I want,' Judge Pearson told me, 'but it won't be more than five years.' My client, Roger Gilbert, thought the plea was satisfactory but wasn't sure he could trust the judge. So Judge Pearson asked me to bring Roger Gilbert into his robing room for the judge's personal assurance. Judge Pearson then repeated his pledge. 'I can sentence you to fifteen years,' he told Gilbert, 'but I don't intend to do so.' At that point, Judge Pearson held up his hand to us, displaying five fingers. Then he leaned back in his chair and told us to trust him. I'll never forget that scene as long as I live. He propped his feet up on his desk and said, 'Trust me, fellas. I have your best interest at heart. Trust me.' And we trusted him."

Barth turns to defendant Roger Gilbert's hearing testimony to check his testimony against Barnes's: "In the judge's robing room," Gilbert had testified, "Judge Pearson said, 'Trust me.' The judge said he wouldn't give me more than five years. And then he raised five fingers. He said, 'I won't tell you what the sentence will be but it won't be more than five years.' And I asked him if he was going to double-cross me and he said again, 'Trust me, trust me.' And I figured, if you can't trust a judge, who can you trust?"

2:00 P.M.

"Judge, is there any particular reason why Judge Talbert wants to clutter up my calendar with another trial this afternoon?" asks George Giles, handing Barth the folder on the defendant scheduled to go to trial.

"George, I'm surprised at you," says Barth. "You should be flattered that Judge Talbert has selected you to participate in this historic quest for justice."

"Sure, Judge, sure. I'm flattered. But I'd be a lot more flattered if he'd do something about my unjustly low salary."

"You have a very bad attitude, George," says Barth with a roguish grin.

As he scans the criminal record of Willie Franklin, the defendant scheduled to go on trial on the charge of rape in the first degree, Barth realizes that he is not dealing with a wayward youth: Franklin is forty-eight years old and has a criminal record dating back to 1939, which includes two convictions for armed robbery. Although he has not been convicted of rape, Franklin has been charged with the crime three times, most recently only a year ago.

Assistant District Attorney Tom Snowden carefully unpacks his briefcase at the prosecutor's table. He is wearing a solid gray suit, maroon tie, black tassel loafers, and steel-rimmed glasses. At thirty-five, Snowden is an elder statesman in the DA's office, since most of the prosecutors leave for more lucrative jobs in private practice before their thirtieth birthdays.

Martin Bowers, the defendant's attorney, is reading his notes at the defense table. He looks older than his thirty-two years because he is bald and wears large, horn-rimmed glasses. His brown tweed jacket adds to his avuncular appearance.

Willie Franklin, who sits next to Bowers, is methodically chewing a large wad of gum. Franklin is a big man with gray-black hair and mustache, a pock-marked face and massive shoulders. He is dressed casually in tan trousers, red shirt, and brown cardigan sweater.

As the prospective jurors file into the courtroom, Snowden and Bowers continue to study their notes, glancing up only occasionally at their jury pool. Like all other jury pools that come into Barth's courtroom, this group gives the appearance of adequately representing a cross-section of the urban community. Over one third are black. There is a sprinkling of what appear to be Oriental-Americans, Spanish-Americans, and

Italian-Americans as well as those whose looks give no clue as to origin.

George Giles spins the wooden wheel on his desk, picks out the slips of the first twelve prospective jurors to be questioned, and asks them to step into the jury box. The interest of the prosecutor and the defense attorney quickens. The two survey each prospective juror's face, searching for some sign that might tell whether to accept or reject.

Barth notices the attorneys' concentration. Uh oh. We may be in for a long afternoon. Mr. Snowden and Mr. Bowers look as if they subscribe to the theory that lawyers can weed out jurors biased against them by skillful questioning. Barth had abandoned that theory years ago. When he had been a practicing trial attorney, Barth became convinced that a lawyer could do as well with the first twelve willing jurors as with any of the others who followed. The biased juror who had wanted to serve could find a way to get on the jury in any case because he would know the right answers to give. As for the others, Barth had not thought that a pseudo-psychological analysis would have come up with one juror who was more likely to be fair or favorable to one attorney's side than the other's. So Barth had asked a few questions to determine if a juror could be open-minded and that was it. Barth still believes in that limited strategy.

"Mr. Rockwell, has any member of your family been a victim of a crime?" asks Snowden. "No." "Do you have any relatives connected with any law-enforcement agencies?" Again, negative. A half-dozen more questions, mostly relating to the prospective juror's ability to be fair-minded, and Snowden sits down.

Barth chides himself. You should be ashamed of yourself, James Barth. Apparently, Mr. Snowden has learned something since he's been in the DA's office. He is brief and to the point. Very promising. Let's see if Mr. Bowers does as well.

"Mr. Rockwell, have you seen any TV programs in which sex crimes are depicted?" "Yes." "Have any of these programs given you any preconceived ideas about sex crimes?" "No." "Have you read any stories about sex crimes in newspapers or magazines that might influence your judgment in a case involving a sex crime here?" "No." "Is there any reason why you think you could not be a fair juror in this case?" "No." "Thank you, Mr. Rockwell."

I'm in luck, Barth is thinking. Mr. Bowers seems as reasonable as Mr. Snowden. These attorneys know they're not going to get perfect jurors. There are prejudices floating around in most people's subconsciouses. But no amount of questioning is going to bring them to the surface. You have to be satisfied to cover the most obvious areas of prejudice and leave it at that. Snowden and Bowers both seem to understand this.

While the two attorneys continue the jury selection, Barth reads the police report in the Franklin case. The defendant, who is black, has been charged with the rape of a black woman in her apartment late one summer night. Both the victim and a neighbor have positively identified Franklin as the attacker. I hope for Mr. Franklin's sake, Barth thinks, that Martin Bowers is an able defense attorney.

Barth looks up from his reading and counts the accepted jurors. Six. All white, so far. Barth suspects that it is Mr. Bowers, representing a black defendant, who is excluding all of the blacks from the jury. And it's probably a very smart move on his part. He figures that law-abiding blacks will be particularly sensitive to a black man stalking a black woman in their neighborhood. They will see Mr. Franklin as a menace to them and their neighbors.

On the other hand, some whites might think that free living and free loving is the way of life in the victim's neighborhood. If Mr. Franklin's attorney can subtly plant that idea in the jurors' minds, he may get an acquittal. That's probably

(111)

Franklin's best chance, and both Franklin and his attorney, Bowers, seem to know it. Franklin has been conferring with Bowers after each black has been questioned. And each black, so far, has been dismissed. That's no coincidence.

At 4:30 Court Officer Alfred Lorenzo walks into the courtroom and passes a note to George Giles. Giles reads it quickly and then delivers it to Barth. It is from the foreman of the Harding jury, who has written out three questions: (1) Does the assault have to be a part of the robbery? (2) Is a fist considered a weapon under the statutory requirement for assault? (3) Can a jury reach a unanimous verdict on some counts and not others?

These questions don't go to the core issue of John Harding's guilt or innocence, Barth reflects. That's probably been decided. But somebody is holding out against the majority. This is a way for the majority to pull in that last juror or two. Instead of bickering over small points, someone is saying to the dissenters, "Have the judge explain it." That lets tempers cool. And my answers may suggest a way for the jury to break the impasse.

Barth decides to call the Harding jury back as soon as the last juror for the Franklin trial has been selected. The judge looks up and counts noses. Attorneys Snowden and Bowers have agreed on twelve jurors. Only one, an interior designer, is black. Ten minutes later, Mrs. Marilyn Porter, a retired elementary school teacher, is sworn in as an alternate. Barth dismisses the newly selected Franklin jury for the day, telling the jurors to return for opening statements in the case tomorrow at 11:30 A.M. Barth then asks Alfred Lorenzo to escort the Harding jury into his courtroom.

After the Harding jurors have returned to the jury box, Barth addresses them: "Ladies and gentlemen of the jury, I have received your note and I will try to answer your questions.

(112)

Number One. Does the assault have to be a part of the robbery? According to the statute, assault in the second degree takes place if the defendant, during the course of a robbery, has caused a physical injury to the victim, in this case to Miss Karen Petersen. So the answer to your question is 'no,' the assault doesn't have to be a part of the robbery but must take place during the commission of the robbery. Second question. Is the fist considered a dangerous weapon within the meaning of the statutory definition of assault in the second degree? The answer is 'no.' The statute defines a dangerous weapon as a gun or sharp object. Obviously, the fist doesn't qualify. Question number three. You have asked if you can reach a unanimous verdict on some counts but not on others. You can, but I prefer that you don't. I urge you to continue your deliberations on all charges with the object of rendering a unanimous verdict on all counts."

That ought to do it, Barth thinks, as he watches the last juror leave his courtroom. It's five now. The jury should have a verdict within the next hour.

5:06 P.M.

Barth aches. Every part of his body—back, legs, eyes—seems to be sending messages to his brain, saying, "It's the end of the day, Barth, so slow down."

Sound advice, Barth tells himself. Dutifully, he closes the door to his chambers and walks to the cabinet containing his modest liquor supply and portable refrigerator. After dropping three ice cubes into a highball glass and pouring Scotch over them, Barth slumps into his desk chair and tells himself to relax. That's what he tells himself, three times, but it doesn't work. The trouble is that he can't shake the Gilbert case. He wants to have his opinion written by Friday and he knows there is a lot of work to be done.

The hearing testimony that he read at lunch of the defendant, Roger Gilbert, and his attorney, Whitney Barnes, had been straightforward enough. Both had said that Judge Pearson promised Gilbert a top of five years in prison in return for a plea of attempted robbery. Barth's thoughts turn to the central figure in the case, Judge Randolph Pearson, and the bizarre events of last Friday:

"Melvin, call Judge Pearson's office and remind him that he is due to testify in my courtroom at two," Barth had said. "I don't want him to claim at the last minute that he's in the middle of transcendental meditation or something and can't make it."

Melvin had returned to Barth's office a few minutes later, his face ashen. "Judge, Pearson's assistant says that he's got a trial on today and that he won't be able to testify."

"You tell Pearson's assistant I'm not taking any shit from Randy Pearson," Barth had shouted. "It's that simple. If he doesn't show at two o'clock, I'll issue a subpoena. He has no business as important as testifying in my courtroom. Aside from duty, I would think that honor would dictate that Randy Pearson appear this afternoon. After all, it's his integrity that has been challenged in my courtroom."

Rich dutifully had followed Barth's orders and, fifteen minutes later, had reappeared in Barth's chambers. "Assistant District Attorney Rollins called," Rich had said. "Pearson's office must have talked to him after my first call. Rollins says that he wants to do everything possible to accommodate Judge Pearson."

"Well, we've done that," Barth had retorted. "Pearson was supposed to testify yesterday. When he said it wasn't convenient, I held it over until today. That's as much accommodation as Randy Pearson or anybody else is entitled to.

"And, Melvin," Barth had growled as his assistant was about to leave his chambers. "Tell Rollins that I view Randy Pearson as just another witness. If he doesn't show up, I'm obliged to make the strongest possible finding against the People. That is a basic rule of evidence. You tell Mr. James Rollins that."

Barth's phone had rung shortly after Melvin's departure. "Judge," Barth's secretary, Betsy, had said, "Mr. Rollins would like to speak to you on line one."

"Yes, sir," Barth had boomed into the receiver. "Ummm. Ummm. Well, you tell Judge Pearson to appear in my court-room at two o'clock this afternoon. That's a direction. Thank you."

When Melvin had returned, Barth had told him to come into his chambers. "Go down to Pearson's courtroom and check his calendar," Barth had said. "If he has a trial, I want to know exactly what kind and what the status of it is. Don't call. Go down there to see for yourself. I don't want to take his clerk's word for anything."

While Barth had been eating lunch in his chambers, Judge Randolph Pearson, tall and elegant in a three-piece pin-striped blue suit, had burst in, unannounced. "I've been informed that you have requested my testimony at two o'clock," Pearson had said stiffly.

Barth had nodded.

"That's impossible," Pearson had said. "I have a trial of my own that has been on for ten days. I want to finish it today."

"Judge Pearson, my legal assistant has informed me that you have a civil trial before a six-man jury. A man's liberty is at stake at my hearing. In addition, the defense attorney in my case has a long-standing obligation to be on trial elsewhere next week and I promised him when this hearing began at the first of the week that he could meet that obligation. Under the circumstances, I think my hearing is more important. Your trial ought to be postponed."

"Look, you can't order me to do anything," Pearson had said angrily. "My court business is as important as yours."

"I have already delayed this hearing a day for your convenience," Barth had replied. "I'm not going to do it again. You are not under subpoena, but you are to appear in my courtroom at two o'clock at my direction."

"I'll let you know of my decision," Pearson had said, storming out of Barth's chambers as abruptly as he had entered.

Sitting at his desk outside Barth's closed door, Melvin had shuddered as he overheard the two judges' argument. After Pearson had left, Melvin cautiously had knocked on Barth's door.

"Come in," Barth had said.

"Judge," Rich had begun quietly, "Pearson has had this trial on for ten days and it looks like he can finish up this afternoon. I know Rollins doesn't want to push Judge Pearson. He wants him to come in at his convenience."

"Let me tell you something, Melvin," Barth had cut in. "Randy Pearson's convenience is never."

"But, Judge," Melvin had said, "it seems to me that Judge Pearson has some rights too. After all, he's got a trial on . . . "

"First of all, Judge Pearson has a civil trial before six jurors. No judge in his right mind is going to wind up a complicated civil case on a Friday afternoon. The jurors have rights, too. They want a free weekend. Frankly, I think Randy Pearson is enough of a faker to have contrived the whole thing. I suspect he manipulated his calendar so that he would be in a position to tell me he couldn't come to testify today. And, of course, once Randy had done this, he didn't think anybody would say 'no' to him. He's been working on that assumption for years. 'But, of course, Randy. Please go ahead with your trial. We'll just sit on our asses and wait until it is convenient for you to testify.' That's the response Randy Pearson expected.

"We have two court proceedings here, Melvin. One cannot go forward. I've decided it's going to be the one in Pearson's courtroom. I don't see anything unreasonable about that.

Roger Gilbert is in jail as a result of a sentence imposed by Judge Pearson. Gilbert says that Judge Pearson promised him a top of five years if he pleaded to attempted armed robbery, a plea which Gilbert took in open court. But Pearson sentenced him to fifteen years. Gilbert says Judge Pearson double-crossed him, and so does Gilbert's lawyer. Answering these charges will, I think, be as serious a matter as Randy Pearson will deal with in his career on the bench. I don't know how Judge Pearson is going to respond to Gilbert's charges, but I'm sure as hell interested in finding out. And today, Melvin, I am going to do everything within my power to find out."

Barth takes another sip of Scotch and shakes his head. That had been the most unusual Friday lunch hour that he had spent since becoming a judge. But it had only been an introduction to the events that unfolded in his courtroom that same afternoon:

At two o'clock last Friday afternoon, Barth had been sitting on the bench, calmly reading the afternoon newspaper as if his demand that Judge Pearson testify in his courtroom had been of no more concern to him than yesterday's horoscope. But those around Barth had not been so casual. Melvin Rich had sat by the side door to the courtroom, blinking nervously and dabbing his perspiring forehead with his handkerchief. Court officers Alfred Lorenzo and Sam Mitchell had stood silently at the jury box railing with their arms folded. Even George Giles, former paratrooper and usually the coolest man in the courtroom, had seemed to feel the pressure of the moment, repeatedly thumbing through his official ledger although all court business for the day—except Judge Pearson's appearance—had long since transpired.

The front door to the courtroom had swung open at 2:01 P.M. and Assistant District Attorney Rollins, alone, had walked down the center aisle. When he had reached the bench, Rollins had announced, "Your Honor, I have conveyed your direction to Judge Pearson."

Before he responded, Barth had motioned to the court reporter to make his words part of the public record. "I am obliged to observe," Barth had begun, "that despite my direction to Judge Pearson to appear at this hearing this afternoon, he has not done so. It seems to me that it comes with ill grace that a trial judge should prevent me from concluding a hearing, particularly when questions of whether a defendant received a fair trial in that trial judge's courtroom and that trial judge's own integrity are at issue. If I were in Judge Pearson's shoes, I would put everything else aside to be here and clear up these questions. Now, if Judge Pearson doesn't want to come here and gives as a pretext that he needs this afternoon to complete a jury trial in a civil case with six jurors, I won't accept that as an excuse."

Barth had stared coldly at Rollins. "How do the People want me to proceed, Mr. Rollins?"

Rollins had shifted his weight uncomfortably from his right foot to his left but had said nothing.

"Well, Mr. Rollins, do the People want to rest their case without Judge Pearson's testimony?"

"We feel, Your Honor, that Judge Pearson should testify so that any misunderstanding that the defendant, Roger Gilbert, had as to his sentence can be cleared up. But we would prefer not to resort to a subpoena of a colleague of yours."

"He's not my colleague," Barth had cut in. "He's a witness. But continue."

"We feel it is demeaning to have another judge appear here against his will. But we feel that Judge Pearson's testimony is essential to show that Gilbert's sentence should not be overturned. If there is no alternative, therefore, we suggest a subpoena."

"Then I will issue a subpoena."

There had been total silence in the courtroom. Barth had actually said that he would subpoena Judge Pearson. Rollins's response had been to look down at the floor, apparently to evade Barth's eyes and the awkwardness of the situation. Finally, Rollins looked up, slowly nodding his head in agreement with Barth.

"Draw up the papers," Barth had ordered. Within five minutes, he had sent Sam Mitchell to Courtroom 35 to deliver a subpoena to the Honorable Randolph Pearson, demanding his immediate presence for testimony in Barth's courtroom.

Barth's courtroom door had opened five minutes later but it had been the city's district attorney, Richard Carter, not Randy Pearson who had entered and approached Barth. "I think, Your Honor, that what I have to say should not be put on the record," Carter had said. "It might save some embarrassment."

"It's a matter of indifference to me whether we save anybody any embarrassment in this case," Barth had replied. "The vice of this entire proceeding, it seems to me, is that there has been too much said and done off the record."

"Your Honor, I have talked to the defense attorney about his commitment for next Monday. I think we may be able to work something out . . . "

"I am not interested in your working something out," Barth had said. "I have a defendant who says he was not given a fair trial. On the present state of the record, if the testimony is not controverted successfully by Judge Pearson, it appears to me that this defendant is entitled to relief. So I see no reason why, in the light of the serious charges against Judge Pearson, he doesn't rush over here to dispose of this matter forthwith."

Carter had attempted a cautious response. "Your Honor, I obviously am in no position to make a judgment on the merits of this case. The situation is an uncomfortable one for all concerned. I wonder if, rather than utilizing a subpoena and risking an awkwardness between judges of coordinate juris-diction, it would be better for us to reach an accommodation that can avoid that awkwardness."

"Nothing that I do by way of a subpoena will affect the relations I have with my colleagues," Barth had replied. "Judge Pearson is no different from any other number of citizens whose occupations we disturb with subpoenas. We sub-poena police officers, doctors, ordinary citizens—and they all lay aside whatever business they have and appear here. Judge Pearson is being asked to do no more than that."

At that moment, George Giles had quietly approached the bench and slipped Barth a note. It had read: "Judge Pearson is on his way over."

Barth takes another sip of Scotch; the memory of forcing a showdown with Randy Pearson on a matter that he had considered important pleases him. But he is disgusted with the way it all had transpired. It had been a perfect example of one of the critical weaknesses of the judicial system: There was no effective check on the power of judges, even when they acted arrogantly and irresponsibly. Randy Pearson had known that he had stepped outside of the boundaries of his official authority when he had refused to appear in Barth's courtroom. But he had figured that he could get away with it. And he had almost succeeded. Everybody from District Attorney Richard Carter on down had tried to step out of his way.

When Pearson finally had appeared, you would have thought he was the God Siva. Everybody was bowing and scraping. While Randy had been nonchalantly tamping down his meerschaum, Carter was on his feet still trying to make Randy comfortable.

"Your Honor," Carter had said, "I would like to say for the record that I understand Judge Pearson was able to arrange to come here. Fortunately, no subpoena had to be served. He is here voluntarily."

After that introduction, Judge Randolph Pearson, while neatly tucking his pipe into his vest pocket, had taken the witness stand. What had followed, Barth recalls, now placing the transcript of Pearson's testimony in front of him for easy reference, had been pretty much a continuation of the Let's-Be-Nice-To-Randy-Pearson Day that the DA's office had been sponsoring.

A flustered James Rollins had begun his examination of Pearson by asking, "Could you, Your Honor, as best you can, recall the facts and circumstances surrounding the plea discussions in the Gilbert case?"

Pearson had paused a moment to indicate he would answer in a way that suited him. "Well, I think discussions began while we were completing arguments on the defense's pre-trial motion to suppress the evidence. I was talking to counsel and I indicated to them that it looked to me like a very close question and could go either way. Under such circumstances, it would seem to me that sensible people ought to talk about what ought to be done." Pearson had paused, then inquired haughtily, "Now what else do you want to know?"

Rollins had struggled through a series of questions which merely established that Pearson had held numerous plea-bargaining sessions with counsel and that all parties agreed to the plea of attempted armed robbery which carried a statutory maximum of fifteen years in prison. Pearson testified that he had made no promise to Gilbert of a five-year sentence. That had been the end of the direct examination.

Carl Elliot, who had represented Gilbert at the hearing, tried to conduct a tough cross-examination but he, like Rollins, had been intimidated by Pearson. "Wasn't it true, Judge Pearson," Elliot had asked, "that both prosecution and defense counsel urged you to decide the pre-trial motion before beginning the trial?"

"They may have."

"Well, Judge Pearson, why then did you begin the trial?"

"I didn't."

"But you began the jury selection while those motions were pending, didn't you?"

"That's true but I do not consider the jury selection the beginning of the trial."

"Isn't it true, Judge Pearson, that Section 256 of the State Code of Criminal Procedure says that the selection of the jury is the beginning of a trial and that all pre-trial motions must be ruled upon before a trial can begin?"

"That is your interpretation, Mr. Elliot," Pearson had responded coolly. "It is not mine."

"Don't you think your decision on the pre-trial suppression motion would have had a great bearing on how the People and the defense would have selected the jury?"

"It might have."

A frustrated Carl Elliot had dropped that line of questioning and had focused on the plea discussions. "When you had the plea-bargaining meetings with counsel, did you ever commit yourself to any specific sentence for Roger Gilbert?"

"I was asked to commit myself to a specific sentence but I told them it was never my practice. Never my practice. Nobody, I told them, was going to dictate what the sentence would be."

Barth leans back in his chair. Randy Pearson certainly knew how to handle those attorneys. He never let Rollins and Elliot forget that he was a judge, even as he had sat on the witness stand and was interrogated by them. The message had been clear: They questioned him closely at their peril, not his. And Randy's intimidating manner had worked.

Suddenly, Barth sits up straight. The Harding jury! They've been out since lunchtime. And I answered their questions an hour and a half ago. I wonder what in the hell is holding them up now? Maybe I've been wrong all along about this case. Maybe it's Harding's alibi that has this jury hung up. Well, obviously, I'm not going to make dinner on time tonight. I'd better let Helen know.

Barth makes the necessary phone call to his wife and then returns to the perusal of the Gilbert case and the transcript of Pearson's testimony at last week's hearing: After both Rollins and Elliot had failed to question Pearson closely, Barth reluctantly had decided he would never have gotten to the bottom of the dispute unless he intervened. So he had jumped into the interrogation, reading verbatim from the previous testimony of Whitney Barnes in which Gilbert's original defense attorney swore that Judge Pearson had promised Gilbert no more than a five-year sentence. "Did any discussion of a five-year term take place?" Barth had asked Pearson.

"Yes," Peason had answered.

"Was any promise of a five-year term made to Roger Gilbert or his attorney, Whitney Barnes?"

"No, not as I understood the discussion," Pearson had replied.

"Not as I understood the discussion," Barth repeats as he continues reading the transcript of Pearson's testimony. Pearson finally admitted that he had discussed a five-year term for Gilbert but he wouldn't be pinned down. He expects me to believe that Whitney Barnes, who has been practicing at this bar for twenty years, and Roger Gilbert, who probably has participated in almost as many plea-bargaining sessions as Barnes, misunderstood him? That Barnes and Gilbert were so naïve that they mistook Pearson's "discussion" of a five-year term for a binding commitment?

The phone rings. George Giles informs Barth that the

Harding jury has a verdict. Barth places the Gilbert transcript in the top drawer of his desk, puts his coat on, and walks quickly to the elevator.

7:03 P.M.

The twelve men and women who make up the Harding jury return to Barth's courtroom, led by the foreman, the blond high school history teacher. They appear fatigued and visibly nervous as they walk directly to the jury box without looking at defendant, counsel, or judge.

"Will the foreman of the jury and the defendant, John Harding, please stand up?" George Giles asks.

The foreman slowly rises from his chair. John Harding stands at the defense table.

"Has the jury reached a verdict, Mr. Foreman?" asks Giles.

"Yes, we have," the foreman replies in a quiet, almost inaudible voice.

"On the first count, grand larceny in the second degree, how do you find the defendant, John Harding?"

"Not guilty."

Barbara Jennings smiles at her client, John Harding. Bob Carlin shifts uncomfortably in his chair at the prosecutor's table. The jury still appears tense and serious.

"On the second count, robbery in the first degree, how do you find the defendant, John Harding?" asks Giles.

"Guilty."

John Harding's body stiffens. Barbara Jennings's smile evaporates.

"On the third count, possession of a dangerous weapon, how do you find the defendant, John Harding?"

"Guilty."

"On the fourth count, assault in the second degree, how do you find the defendant, John Harding?"

"Guilty."

Barbara Jennings's voice trembles as she asks for a poll of the jury. As each member of the jury endorses the unanimous verdict, John Harding stares down at the defense table. Prosecutor Bob Carlin smiles at each juror appreciatively.

"Ladies and gentlemen of the jury," says Barth. "I want to thank you for performing your duty. You are now free to go."

As the jurors by twos and threes move uneasily toward the courtroom door, Alfred Lorenzo and Sam Mitchell silently step up to flank John Harding. The officers' impassive expressions, cultivated over the bureaucratic years, contrast with the look of quiet desperation in young John Harding's eyes. The defendant is totally alone now, moved like a filing cabinet, to temporary storage in the city jail.

"I can understand the verdict," George Giles says to Barth, "but I don't understand why it took the jury so long."

"My hunch," replies Barth, "is that all but one or two of the jurors wanted to find Harding guilty on all counts, including the grand larceny. But there were one or two who balked. So whoever assumed leadership in the group started looking for a compromise. That's what took so long. They finally gave the dissenters the single not guilty count and that satisfied everybody.

"But it was a good verdict, George," Barth adds. "There was very little evidence that John Harding took that twenty-four hundred dollars from the safe. Carlin had the testimony of Karen Petersen and Mrs. Mendoza and that's it. No cafeteria accounts or receipts of any kind."

"So what are you going to do with John Harding?" asks Giles.

"I wish I knew," Barth replies. "I wish I knew."

IV

Thursday

7:15 A.M.

Horace Conrad steps off the freight elevator with his janitor's broom and walks down the empty corridor to Court-room 27. He has taken this same walk every weekday morning for the last eighteen years. Little has changed in those years except the names framed under glass to the right of the court-room entrance. Today, the name is Judge James Barth. Six years ago, it was Judge George Harwood, and before that, Judge Hollis Brownell. Conrad has never met a judge but assumes that most of them are bearded and wise, like Moses.

After he enters the courtroom, Conrad pauses, out of respect, at the wooden railing separating the public gallery from the trial area. He reads the motto, IN GOD WE TRUST, that is lettered above the elevated bench. He likes the motto. The words make him think about his service in the Baptist church and his devotion to God.

His tranquility is destroyed as soon as he begins dusting the defense table. He finds a newly carved plea, "Kathleen: where are you?" on the lower frame. A black scorch mark is still there, a result, one of the court officers once told Conrad, of an attempt by one defendant to burn down the courtroom with toilet paper and a match he had secretly smuggled in. Conrad shakes his head in dismay.

He brightens up as he moves across the aisle to the prosecutor's table, which has no carvings or scorch marks. As he dusts it, he feels that he is doing his small part to help the district attorney fight the criminal element. Feeling particularly bold today, Conrad walks to the bench and sits in the judge's chair. Suddenly, he stands up straight, spreads his arms grandly and waits for the divine inspiration that he assumes comes to Judge James Barth every weekday morning.

Barth lies in bed, waiting for sleep that he now knows will not come. He has been tossing uncomfortably for the last forty-five minutes, reviewing basketball scores, weather reports, commodity futures—anything to take his mind off the one subject that has kept him awake and anxious most of the night: John Harding. But nothing works. What is the "correct" sentence, he keeps asking himself, for this twenty-four-year-old man, now convicted of assault and armed robbery in the first degree? Would twenty-five years in the state penitentiary do Harding or anybody else any good? Would fifteen years make any more sense? Oh, to hell with this numbers game, Barth grumbles.

He gets up slowly, walks into the dining room, and sits down in a chair at the mahogany table. Over the fireplace, Helen peers down from the portrait painted after her law school graduation. So serene, so beautiful, he thinks. Helen. She'll sleep another thirty minutes, dress, and at nine o'clock walk into the firm of Hastings and Hastings for another intensive day of counseling clients on their tax problems. Tax law provides the perfect intellectual arena for Helen's mind. Precise, analytical, practical in a particularly cerebral way.

He knew that he would be no match for Helen in the tax field. He doesn't have the temperament to hunt for exemptions and deductions in the Internal Revenue Code every weekday morning. No, he has always preferred the flesh and blood of the law, the people who always clutter up statutes and codes with their untidy problems. People like John Harding and Roger Gilbert. . . . What he needs this morning, he decides, is a special treat, something that will lift him out of his lousy mood.

Barth snaps his fingers. Suddenly, he rushes to his study and returns with a manila folder labeled "Truman Interview—1957." He opens the folder to notes dated May 18, 1957, scribbled hurriedly after he had returned from an out-of-town trip. That extraordinary day had begun routinely enough with Barth taking a taxi to the station to catch a 6:30 A.M. train. As he approached the station, Barth noticed that a crowd had gathered and learned that a man he greatly admired, Harry Truman, was taking the same train.

After he stepped aboard the parlor car, Barth had made his way to seat number three. To his surprise and delight, he found that Harry Truman occupied the seat next to his. There were only two other passengers, both at the opposite end of the car. Must be Republicans, Barth had decided.

"Mr. President, I know you're busy," Barth had said. "I don't want to disturb you."

"You won't disturb me," Truman had snapped. And that had been the beginning of a conversation that lasted the entire length of the trip.

The record of this conversation is contained in squiggly notes on several sheets of yellow paper. "HST won't talk about politics. Will talk about C. Daniel family. Shows grandchildren's pictures—Discusses sale of presidential papers. Jefferson family sold papers to Princeton for $250,000. HST thinks this wrong. Considers presidential papers public documents—Glances at morning paper. Curses columnist. Says he doesn't know how anyone can think he can be interesting everyday of the week—HST wonders whether people 5,000 years from now will study American cities as others have studied Pompeii. Wonders what they'll think about our cities—Discusses raising children in the White House. HST never spanked Margaret. Bess did."

In his conversation with Barth, Truman had referred to his wife as "the boss." He had emphasized his respect for her formidable temper with an anecdote: He and Margaret, his daughter, were having lunch in the White House alone one day when they began a friendly argument. Before long, the two were gleefully spitting watermelon seeds at each other. At the height of the battle, Bess Truman walked into the White House dining room. "Harry Truman," she bellowed. "That's no way for the President of the United States to act." The nation's thirty-third President sheepishly withdrew from the line of battle, as he said he always did when "the boss" laid down the law.

Barth chuckles. He loves that story. And that train trip was just about the most memorable he had ever taken. He looks at his watch and realizes that he must leave his pleasant memories. It is time for his daily metamorphosis into the Honorable James Barth, State Criminal Court Judge.

8:35 A.M.

Barth carefully stacks the folders of the day's defendants on his desk and picks up the one on top. It is sentencing day for Ronald Hartwell, who has pleaded guilty to possession of a weapon. On the face of it, Hartwell's crime was no big deal. He was carrying a piece. Nobody got hurt. As he reviews

Hartwell's pre-sentencing report, however, Barth becomes increasingly concerned.

First of all, unlike many of Barth's black and Puerto Rican defendants, Hartwell cannot plead poverty and prejudice as the root of his problem and record. He was brought up in a white, lower-middle-class home and attended parochial schools through one term of college. On a 1960 I.Q. test, Hartwell scored an impressive 132. According to his parents, "Ronald has always respected his elders and has always been a hard worker."

What troubles Barth is the work Hartwell has chosen to perform so diligently. He is listed as the operator of concessions at the Continental Health Spa, probably a front for a high-priced whorehouse, and his weekly salary is $450. That's a lot of dough for selling health foods. Could it be that Mr. Hartwell also gets a cut of the serious action? A reasonable assumption, particularly since only a year ago, Hartwell was arrested and charged with maintaining a house of prostitution. After conviction, Hartwell was put on probation.

Barth considers Hartwell's current problem: On October 26, 1973, at 3:55 A.M., a hotel clerk in the city's red light district observed the defendant, holding a silver pistol, with a female companion in a car outside the hotel. Moments later, the clerk heard shots and called the police. When the police arrived, they found Hartwell in the car, still holding the silver pistol. Hartwell told the cops that the gun belonged to a friend. He said he always "borrowed" a gun for protection when he came to that part of town.

Flogging would be the best sentence in this case, Barth reflects, but they won't allow it anymore. Too bad. Another probationary sentence might do some good, that is, if Mr. Hartwell had a steady job in a sardine cannery. But he's a big-time whorehouse operator who obviously thinks he can make his own rules. After all, he thought nothing of violating probation by proselytizing in the red light district and putting on his little fireworks display. Probation's out. A fine? He'd cover that with the take from one good night's work from his girls. But will prison really do Hartwell any good? Certainly, no rational person believes that prison will rehabilitate Hartwell or anybody else.

I wonder what Harvard Professor James Q. Wilson would do with Mr. Hartwell? Professor Wilson has no problem committing hardened criminals to prison. He says, at the very least, it takes them out of commission temporarily. But Hartwell falls somewhere in between the hardened criminal and the first-timer. There's no satisfactory solution, but I'll settle for a prison term. It's not going to make Mr. Hartwell a candidate for the priesthood but it might jolt him just enough to keep him out of trouble for a while.

Lowell Paul Evans, the defendant whose folder Barth has in his hands next, had spent eight of his twenty-nine years at the Hurst Department Store as a salesman in the store's men's furnishings department. During those eight years, Evans had managed to make a modest living for himself and his family. But his salary increases (three in eight years) had not kept up with inflation. Moreover, Evans had seen younger and newer salesmen come in and sell more, get bigger raises, and then go on to higher positions with the company.

In his frustration, Lowell Evans decided to break the rules, something he had never done before either in school or at work. Every Wednesday night for six weeks, Evans slipped into his department supervisor's office, took out the ledger that recorded each employee's sales for the week and doctored the figures. At first, Evans was cautious, changing $50 purchases to $80 purchases. But as the weeks went by and he remained undetected, he became bolder so that $10 became $90 and $50 was changed to $500. Evans's hope was that the store manager would notice his spiraling sales and promote him. The manager noticed the spiraling figures, but instead of promoting Evans, he had him arrested for falsifying business records.

Barth considers Evans's crime: This was Evans's rather pathetic attempt to impress his boss with his salesmanship. He shouldn't have done it, but everybody can be pardoned a single excess (Evans has no criminal record). Evans is not a criminal and should not be in jail. But I'll have to get Assistant District Attorney Robert Levitt's agreement to a misdemeanor before I can fine Lowell Evans and send him home. Levitt may be a problem. When he's in a bad mood, he treats every case like a Murder One. If Levitt is in one of those obstinate moods today, I'll have to lean on him pretty hard.

Why do I care about Lowell Evans? I'd like to think it's because I'm such a decent, compassionate human being. But I know that's not quite an accurate analysis. Face it, Barth, you're a prisoner of your own middle-class values, and Lowell Evans is somebody you can relate to. He's not a rapist or thief or murderer. He's not a whorehouse operator like Ronald Hartwell either. No, Lowell Evans is a man who has tried to make an honest wage for himself and his family all of his adult life. He's had anxieties like most other blue- and white-collar workers: fear of failure, insecurity about his future, a desire to break loose from the shackles of a humdrum job. And he made a mistake. But it's a mistake I can understand and empathize with. There may be a double standard in my courtroom, but it's not based on class distinctions. I'll give both poor and middle-class defendants who are threats to the law-abiding community equal time in prison. Lowell Evans is different. It doesn't matter whether he's poor or middle class. He's no threat to the rest of us. So I'll fight to keep him out of prison.

Barth reaches for the next folder. The name Robert Alton is

printed in blue ink on the cover. The defendant is male, black, thirty-seven years old, unmarried, and convicted of armed robbery in the first degree.

The case is still vivid in Barth's mind, since he presided over Alton's trial only a month ago. Why Alton insisted on going to trial is still a mystery to Barth. He was arrested two blocks away from the bar that had been held up, only five minutes after police received the call reporting the robbery. Three witnesses provided an exact description of Alton, first to police and later to the jury. When arrested, Alton was carrying a .32-caliber automatic in his coat pocket, precisely the weapon, the bartender said, that was brandished in the bar during the robbery.

Alton's attorney made attempts to trip up the prosecution's witnesses in cross-examination at the trial but, when those attempts failed, he had very little to fall back on. He could have put Alton on the witness stand and had him repeat the alibi he had told police—that he was at his sister's apartment at the time of the robbery. The trouble with that strategy would have been that there was no one—Alton's sister or anybody else—whom the defense could produce to corroborate the alibi. Alton's attorney decided that the advantage of putting Alton alone on the stand to give his alibi was outweighed by the disadvantages of the prosecutor then being able to attack Alton's rich and varied criminal record.

That record now faces Barth in the form of three single-spaced typewritten pages beginning, chronologically, in 1954, when Alton was charged with petty theft. Since that time, he has been convicted of possession of drugs, grand larceny, violation of parole, and armed robbery (twice).

The probation department has provided Barth with its report on Robert Alton's background and potential, based largely on a probation officer's interview with the defendant. The probation officer could not find a single member of Alton's family, including the sister who, according to Alton, was with him at the time of the armed robbery. Robert Alton, the probation officer has written, comes from a broken home and has not seen either of his parents in eight years. He left school after sixth grade, has exhibited no employable skill, and, as far as the probation department can determine, has no verifiable employment record. The probation officer has concluded that Robert Alton is "an immature, inadequate individual who has become thoroughly adjusted to a criminal way of life and addicted to drugs seemingly as a means of escaping any confrontation with his problems. Additionally, he has proven his inability in the past to profit from supervision and attempts to help him with his difficulties."

Barth props his elbows on the desk and lets his chin rest in his hands. Now what am I going to do with Robert Alton, he asks himself? Here is a man who fits all the clichés embraced by both liberals and law-and-order conservatives. The liberals can say that Alton grew up in poverty and unhappiness, that society—not Robert Alton—is primarily to blame for his life of crime. The conservatives can point out that, regardless of society's neglect of Robert Alton, the unalterable fact is that the defendant is a danger to law-abiding citizens.

The politicians can make of Robert Alton what they want. In the meantime, I'm the guy who has to decide what to do with him. I suppose I could put him in a drug program and hope that he'll come out of it an ex-addict and solid citizen. The trouble is I don't believe it. The programs that I know about, like Sunshine House, do nothing for the addict except switch him from heroin to methadone. So who gains? Maybe the director of the program, who has a new client and another reason to ask for more government funds. But not Robert Alton, who, when he graduates from the program, will more than likely go back to his old ways. That's happened before.

If I send him upstate, can I expect anything better? He'll

make mattresses and attend a fifth-grade English class once a week. He'll also swap tales and criminal techniques with pals he hasn't seen since the last time they did time together. That's no good either.

There are no good choices, no easy decisions that I know will work. If my only responsibility were to Robert Alton, I probably would gamble with a drug program or light sentence and hope that Alton would, for the first time, straighten himself out. But Robert Alton is not my client. The public is. The fact is I'm paid by the state to protect the public's interests and those interests do not necessarily coincide with Alton's.

My hunch is that if I give Alton a break, he'll get right back in trouble as he has every time in the past. And he may hurt somebody. That's my concern and responsibility. I can't take the chance. Robert Alton has to go back upstate for a long stretch. That's not the kind of decision that inspires anybody, including me. But, realistically, I think it's the only option open to me. Alton is thirty-seven now. The best hope, I'm afraid, is that he will burn out by the time he's fifty. If he's lucky, he may end up in a welfare hotel watching the tube all day.

Barth is down to the last folder, Jesse Norwood's. According to the pre-pleading report, Norwood, who is charged with arson in the first degree, set fire to curtains in his welfare hotel room. When he couldn't put the fire out, he went downstairs and reported it to the manager. As Norwood's reward for confessing error, the manager turned him in to the cops.

Putting a match to a bedroom curtain is not my way of venting frustrations, Barth reflects, but it seems to be Mr. Norwood's. If I had his problems, I might do the same thing. I wish Mel Garment were still in the DA's office. He could have sized this case up in two minutes and I'd never have seen it. It's criminal mischief at best, and Mel would have known it, taken it to the lower court and slapped a ninety-day sentence on Norwood. But, no, some young Turk in the DA's office wants to show his stuff, and all of us, most of all Jesse Norwood, must suffer.

Barth reads on. Norwood was honorably discharged from the navy ten years ago. That's good. He's been hospitalized twice since then for mental problems, the last time five years ago when he told doctors that he heard voices threatening him. That's bad. Norwood may be a bit psycho. At least he's not hurting anybody these days but himself. But can I justify letting Norwood go, now that I'm aware of his mental problems? On the other hand, can I justify keeping him in jail, knowing that his crime is worth no more than a misdemeanor plea and time served?

If I give Norwood a break, will I see him back in court on a more serious charge next time?

The calculated gamble. That's what this business of plea bargaining and sentencing is all about. I didn't prepare for that aspect of my job in the law school classroom. I decide what to do with Mr. Norwood by studying criminal records, not criminological treatises. And I try to take a careful reading of the odds, as careful, that is, as I can be with the few minutes I have for each case. Even if I had more time, would it make any difference? Would it really matter if I had hours to devote to Jesse Norwood? I don't think so. I can only study the information available, and the information available is a probation department report providing only the sketchiest outlines of a human being. And even if I could know everything about Norwood I'd still be left with three inadequate choices: probation, parole, or prison. So I've got an impossible job. And since it's impossible, there is no way for me or anybody else on the bench to be "competent" in judging Jesse Norwood. But if I don't try to do it, somebody else, less concerned than I think I am, will do it.

Assistant District Attorney Robert Levitt, all business and bustle, hurries into Courtroom 27 and deposits his folders on the prosecutor's table. Across the aisle is Attorney Owen Bachrach, already tired this morning, as he has been for all of his twenty-five years of moving poor defendants in and out of courtrooms. Bachrach is memorizing the name of Jesse Norwood and the fact that the defendant has been charged with arson in the first degree for setting a hotel curtain on fire.

Norwood, a slender man with a goatee and long, disheveled brown hair, is escorted to the defense table. He waves Bachrach away from him.

"Let me talk," Norwood says angrily. "Now, Judge, I did this . . . "

Bachrach tries to restrain his client. Then he addresses Barth apologetically. "Your Honor, my client . . . "

"Now wait a minute," Norwood blurts out. "I don't want to be babied. I did it. But I don't want to go back to that jail. That's a bad place, Judge. There are killers in there. I can get hurt. I don't want to go back to that filthy pen, Judge. But I can take four years. I'm a man. I can take four years if that's the decision. I just want a decision, Judge."

Norwood pauses. Bachrach takes advantage of the opportunity. "Your Honor, I ask that the defendant's remarks be stricken from the record."

"This is not a matter of record for a trial, Mr. Bachrach," Barth says, then turns to the defendant. "Mr. Norwood, let me assure you that your attorney and I are capable of making decisions."

"Judge, I'm not talking about my attorney. I'm talking about you, Judge. I can take four years. I'm a man. I just want a decision."

"Mr. Norwood, I don't want to give you four years."

"I don't want to be in that jail, Judge. I'm not a murderer and don't want to be with murderers . . . "

"Mr. Norwood . . . "

"Just give me a chance to speak, Judge. That jail can get a man in trouble. I'd like to be transferred . . . "

Norwood's attorney, Owen Bachrach, tries to interrupt. But Norwood cuts him short.

"Just give me a chance. I got some sense, too."

"May we approach, Your Honor?" asks Bachrach. Barth nods. Bachrach and Robert Levitt move up to the bench. Norwood keeps his eyes fastened on Barth as the three confer.

"Judge," says Levitt, "I'm uneasy about this case. I don't think Norwood is quite all there."

"I agree," Barth says. "But I'm not going to hold that against him. If we put all the psychos in jail, we'd certainly solve the housing problem. But I'm not sure there are enough jails in the entire country to hold them all. Norwood set fire to some curtains in his room and reported it. I just can't get very excited about this. It should have been settled downstairs. But we've got it here, so what are we going to do about it?"

Levitt is silent.

"Is there any way we can put him in a psychiatric unit?" asks Bachrach.

"They'll send him to Tremont," Barth replies. "That's no bargain. If you gentlemen agree to a misdemeanor, I'll parole him for a month before sentencing so he can get some outside treatment."

Bachrach quickly agrees. Levitt nods his head slowly. Then he says, "But he may do something else if he's paroled."

"That's the chance we take, Mr. Levitt," replies Barth.

The conference over, Bachrach walks to the defense table to discuss the plea with Norwood. The defendant turns toward Barth while Bachrach is still explaining the plea to him.

"I really hate talking like this, Judge," says Norwood. "But you don't understand that jail."

"I understand you, Mr. Norwood. We've got something worked out."

"At this time, Your Honor," Bachrach says, "the defendant wishes to withdraw his not guilty plea and plead guilty to the second count of the indictment, criminal mischief, a misdemeanor."

"Mr. Norwood," says Barth "you've had a chance to talk to Mr. Bachrach. You understand that you are pleading guilty to criminal mischief. That means you are admitting you damaged someone else's property . . . "

"But with no intention of hurting anybody, Judge," Norwood interjects.

"I'm aware of that. I'm going to parole you."

"Thank you, Your Honor," Norwood says gratefully.

Barth sets the sentence date for the thirteenth of May and says that Norwood is to be on parole until then.

"The People take exception to the parole," Levitt says evenly.

"In view of the fact that this defendant has been incarcerated for four and a half months," Barth responds, "the parole is justified. The defendant will be sentenced on May thirteenth."

"Mr. Norwood, you understand that you must be in the courtroom on May thirteenth," Giles says.

"I'd be a fool not to after the way the court has treated me today," Norwood says, picking up his coat and heading for the door.

He made his point, Barth is thinking, as he watches Norwood leave. He mentally reviews Norwood's record. True, he's been hospitalized twice. He's heard voices and has thought people were after him. But nothing like that has been reported in the last five years. The only reason he's before me is because he set fire to some curtains. And that is the only problem I have to deal with.

A pale young man dressed in an expensive black suit and white silk tie enters the the courtroom. He spots an equally well dressed older man and sits down next to him. They chat amiably, punctuating their casual conversation with occasional soft laughter. Barth senses instinctively that the younger man must be Ronald Hartwell, operator of the concession stand at the Continental Health Spa, and that his older companion is his high-priced lawyer.

After Hartwell is called forward for sentencing for the crime of possession of a dangerous weapon, the defendant's attorney tells Barth of Hartwell's high intelligence and good education, his Catholic upbringing and loving parents. He draws a verbal picture of a callow youth, struggling for maturity and knowledge in a hostile world. Through the evil influences of others, the attorney says, his voice rising to convey the heavy emotional import of his words, the defendant has gone astray. His arrests are but temporary departures from an otherwise righteous life. The defendant has assured his parents as well as his attorney that he will not get into trouble again. The attorney concludes with the request that Ronald Hartwell be given another probationary sentence.

Barth asks first the defendant and then the DA if either wishes to speak before sentence. Both decline.

"Mr. Hartwell," says Barth, "you have been brought up by parents who care about you. You are very intelligent and have been provided with a good education. You have recently gotten yourself into trouble. You were convicted of maintaining a house of prostitution and given a probationary sentence. You, apparently, did not take that warning seriously. If you had, you would not be here today.

(143)

"I believe the statute under which you were charged and have pleaded guilty was designed for persons such as yourself. That is, for people who think that carrying a loaded weapon on our streets and shooting it off at will is a reasonable way to behave. It is not. Our statute, which makes such behavior a felony, underscores that view. I don't think that there's any point in giving you another term of probation. The sentence of the court is one year in jail."

When Barth announces the jail term, the mouths of Hartwell and his attorney sag in disbelief. George Giles tells them that they have thirty days to appeal the sentence. But they do not appear to hear as they slowly leave the courtroom.

Barth notices a dour, heavyset man wearing a full walrus mustache and frayed olive-green suit. It is Robert Alton's attorney, Herbert Thornhill. "Mr. Giles, call the Alton case," Barth orders.

Robert Alton, stocky and worn-looking beyond his thirty-seven years, steps to the defense table. He offers a tired greeting to his lawyer.

"Is your name Robert Alton," asks Giles, "and is Herbert Thornhill, next to you, your attorney?"

"Yes," says the defendant.

"Mr. Alton, you are here convicted of armed robbery in the first degree. Do the People wish to be heard relative to sentence in this case?"

"No, Your Honor," replies Assistant District Attorney Levitt.

"Mr. Alton," says Giles, "it is your right as well as your attorney's to make a statement at this time."

"Your Honor, I would like to make a statement," Thornhill replies in a deep, languid voice.

"Go ahead, Mr. Thornhill."

"Your Honor, it is sad to think that of my client's thirty-

(144)

seven years, he has spent almost half in prison. I think the blame may lie someplace other than with the defendant. It may reflect something about our society. What do we do with our poor and troubled citizens? We put them in prisons where they are supposed to be rehabilitated. But are they? I have asked Robert what he can do. He told me that he could make license plates and mattresses. These are the skills he has learned in prison. I suggest that this is not enough. I submit that something is missing in the rehabilitation of this man.

"In this case, there was no violence," Thornhill continues. "Mr. Alton was not in that bar to hurt anybody. Under the circumstances, Your Honor, I hope that the court will show some mercy in the interest of justice. I hope you, somehow, will find a way to administer justice in a constructive way. That is all I have to say, Your Honor."

"Mr. Alton, would you like to say something?" Barth asks.

"Your Honor," says the defendant, speaking in quick, nervous phrases, "it just seems to me that justice in this country is one-sided. Poor people don't get it. But Agnew and Nixon do okay. I don't know. I think there has to be a change. That's all I have to say."

Barth measures Alton with a steady gaze. He pauses before addressing the defendant. "Mr. Alton, you have a three-page yellow sheet which includes two convictions for armed robbery and one for grand larceny. This is your fifth felony conviction. Nobody forced you into committing this crime. This was a stickup which you alone were responsible for. You speak of justice and say that poor people never receive it. Well, there are a lot of poor people, unlike you, who work hard to make an honest living. Your victim in this stickup was trying to make a living and so were your other victims. They want justice, too. Somebody has to protect them from you.

"You mention Mr. Agnew and Mr. Nixon, that this one-sided system of justice seems to treat them differently from you.

I couldn't agree with you more. I wish Mr. Agnew and Mr. Nixon were in my courtroom. If they were, I can assure you they would be treated no differently from you. But you are in my courtroom, Mr. Alton, and I must deal with you. You are sentenced to the state prison for a term not to exceed fifteen years."

Alton shakes his head dejectedly as George Giles advises him of his right to appeal the sentence within thirty days. *I don't blame you for being discouraged,* Barth is thinking. *You haven't had many breaks along the way and, maybe, if you had, you wouldn't be here today. But you've got to try to see it from my point of view, Mr. Alton. If I let you out early, I may have to answer to your next victim, if he's alive to argue with me.*

The next case on Barth's calendar is that of Lowell Evans, the salesman who wanted to impress his superiors with his skill and merchandise orders. Lowell Evans stands at the counsel table, a small, clean-shaven man who wears thick glasses and is wrapped in an ill-fitting blue blazer.

"We can offer a plea of falsification of business records," Prosecutor Levitt says, opening the bidding.

Barth shoots him an incredulous look, but says nothing.

"I don't want to go to trial," sighs Evans's lawyer. "But you're trying to squeeze me here. I'd rather go to trial than take that plea. Judge, my client is twenty-nine years old. He's been a salesman for eight years and has never been in trouble before. This was a mistake. He admits it. But I don't think it's worth a felony."

Barth listens intently and slowly nods his head in agreement. But he doesn't say anything immediately. "He's got a point," Barth says finally. "Evans is no bum. He's a salesman who got a little too ambitious. I don't really see the need to stick him with a felony conviction. What do you think, Mr. Levitt?"

Levitt senses the subtle pressure Barth is putting on him to offer the misdemeanor plea. He needs one more push. "Come on, Bob," says Barth. "You've got a big job and a lot better things to spend your time on than this little case."

"All right, Judge. I'll make it a misdemeanor. But I'm not happy about it."

"Nobody's paying you to be happy, Mr. Levitt," says Barth. "George," he says gleefully to his clerk, "would you please take Mr. Evans's plea."

11:34 A.M.

Barth shifts mental gears from the case of Lowell Evans to the upcoming legal fortunes of Willie Franklin. His reading of the police report and Franklin's record and his observation of Franklin's attorney's effort to systematically exclude blacks from the jury suggests that Franklin is guilty of burglary, petty larceny and rape, as charged. So what happens, assuming that Franklin is, in fact, guilty, if the jury votes for acquittal? Will justice have been served? If there is an acquittal, I hope my response will be affirmative. I hope that I'll accept the legally sanctioned judgment of twelve jurors as a fair and, therefore, just decision. That's how I *hope* I'll respond. But whether I will respond that way may be another matter. . .

Barth's idle speculations end abruptly when George Giles informs him that the Franklin jury is assembled and ready to enter the courtroom. Already Prosecutor Tom Snowden and Defense Attorney Martin Bowers have taken their seats at the counsel tables. Next to Bowers the defendant, Willie Franklin, dressed again in brown cardigan sweater and tan corduroy pants, appears relaxed. Court Officer Alfred Lorenzo leads the twelve jurors and Mrs. Marilyn Porter, the retired elementary school teacher who serves as alternate, to their places.

After Giles has formally announced the continuation of the

Franklin trial, Barth says, "You may begin with your opening statement, Mr. Snowden."

The prosecutor, dressed in the same gray suit that he wore yesterday, rises, takes a last look at his notes, and walks quickly to the railing in front of the jury.

"Ladies and gentlemen of the jury," Snowden begins, "what I am going to present to you now is a preview of what I will prove when I begin to submit evidence in this case of the People versus Willie Franklin. This is the opening statement. It is like the cover on a jigsaw puzzle.

"The defendant, Willie Franklin, is charged with burglary, petty larceny, and rape in the first degree," says Snowden, speaking earnestly but without emotion. "I am going to submit evidence to prove the following set of facts. At about eleven thirty P.M. on the night of July 17, 1973, Mrs. Delores Harper closed the box office at the downtown Rivoli movie theater, where she works as a cashier. As she does every night that she works, Mrs. Harper walked six blocks to the bus stop at the corner of First and Main Streets and waited for her friend, Leroy Armstrong. When Mr. Armstrong did not appear, Mrs. Harper boarded the bus alone.

"At approximately midnight, Mrs. Harper got off the bus at the corner of Grove and Lancaster Streets and walked six blocks to her apartment house at 311 Grove Street. After Mrs. Harper opened the front door, she felt an arm around her neck. Mrs. Harper looked around and saw the defendant, Willie Franklin.

" 'Don't scream,' said Franklin. Terrified, Mrs. Harper said nothing. She tried to pull free. But Willie Franklin, who, as you can see, is a large man, held her tight. 'Don't fight,' Franklin said to Mrs. Harper, 'because it doesn't matter. I'm going to fuck you.'

"With that threat, Willie Franklin, keeping a stranglehold on Mrs. Harper, forced her up the steps to her third-floor apartment. Before entering, Franklin asked Mrs. Harper, 'Is your boyfriend home?' She replied, 'He might be.' Franklin ignored her answer. 'It doesn't matter,' he said.

"After Franklin had forced his way into Mrs. Harper's apartment, he pushed Mrs. Harper into the bedroom and ordered her to take off her clothes. She refused. Franklin then pulled off her blouse and slacks. 'Take off the rest,' he said. She refused. Willie Franklin ripped off Mrs. Harper's bra and panties and threw them on the floor.

"Franklin ordered her to lie on the bed. She refused. 'Do what I say, woman,' he said. 'It'll be better for both of us.' Still Delores Harper would not lie down. So the defendant threw her on the bed. And he forced her legs apart, despite her resistance. Then he forced his penis into Delores Harper's vagina and had sexual intercourse with her."

Snowden is telling the story without any noticeable effort to inflame the jury. He has only raised his voice once, so far, when he told the jury of Willie Franklin's statement, "I'm going to fuck you." But even then, Snowden gave the impression he was reciting an oft-told story. The Franklin case is a job for veteran prosecutor Tom Snowden, not a cause.

"Willie Franklin left Mrs. Harper on her bed, crying hysterically," Snowden continues. "The defendant then took five dollars from Mrs. Harper's purse, picked up a fan and pillow from the bedroom and ran out the door. When Franklin shut the door, Delores Harper screamed. The screams were heard by Charles Mapes, who lives on the second floor of the apartment house. Mapes ran into the hall.

"'Hey, Racket, what are you doing?' asked Mapes, who recognized Franklin and knew his street name, Racket. Franklin told Mapes that he had met Mrs. Harper at a bar. But when Mapes asked Franklin why he was carrying a fan and pillow, Franklin suddenly ran down the steps and out the front door.

(149)

"As Franklin was running out the front door, Delores Harper burst out of her apartment screaming that she'd been attacked. Mapes decided to help Mrs. Harper rather than chase Franklin. The next day Delores Harper went to Harris Hospital for treatment. After her release, she reported the crime to the police.

"Six days later, on July twenty-fourth, Mrs. Harper and her boyfriend, Leroy Armstrong, were shopping on Grove Street. Mrs. Harper spotted the defendant talking to another man. She did not want to tell Mr. Armstrong, fearing that he and Franklin would get into a fight and Mr. Armstrong might get hurt. Instead, Mrs. Harper found a telephone and called the police. When Detectives William Farrell and Peter Carlson arrived, Mrs. Harper identified Willie Franklin as the man who had attacked her. Franklin was arrested and charged with burglary, petty larceny, and rape in the first degree.

"Those are the facts, ladies and gentlemen. Those are the pieces of the jigsaw puzzle. During this trial I am going to present evidence to back each and every detail that I have told you this morning. Taken together, they will present the whole picture of the crimes committed by the defendant, Willie Franklin. Thank you for your attention."

While Snowden has been blocking out the charges against Willie Franklin, Martin Bowers, Franklin's attorney, has been writing notes on a pad of paper. After Snowden has finished, Bowers rises and faces Barth.

"Your Honor, the defense waives an opening statement," he says.

"All right," Barth replies, looking at the courtroom clock. "Let's break for lunch and return at two. Mr. Snowden, have your first witness ready to testify then."

It's not surprising that Martin Bowers waived the defense's opening statement, Barth reflects as he walks to the elevator. I doubt that Bowers will put Willie Franklin on the stand. If he does, he knows that the prosecutor will attack Franklin's record, including his earlier arrests on charges of rape. No, Mr. Bowers's defense will succeed or fail on the strength of his cross-examination of the prosecution's witnesses.

12:46 P.M.

"What's up, Betsy?" asks Barth, after he returns to his office.

"Judge Jackson called. She wants to know if you're busy for lunch today. Nothing else."

Barth reaches for the phone and dials a number. "This is Judge Barth. Is Judge Jackson there? . . . Thank you. . . . Mary? How are you? . . . Good. I'll meet you at the front entrance in ten minutes."

Barth purposely arrives at the courthouse steps a few minutes early so that he can inhale the mild, spring air. It will be good to see Mary, he thinks as he waits for his luncheon companion. He has not seen much of Mary Jackson since that murder trial five years ago. Then she wasn't Judge Jackson, but Mary Jackson, defense attorney. And what a defense attorney! Barth had never witnessed a better performance. She practically had the DA on his knees begging for mercy by the end. After that trial, Barth had decided if he ever had a legal problem, he would hire Mary Jackson.

A gaunt, bespectacled woman in her late forties waves to Barth from a few yards away. Barth holds out both hands in greeting, then gives Mary Jackson a big hug.

"Hello, Mary. How've you been?"

"Fine, just fine, Jim. Gosh, it's good to see you. How's the family?"

"Oh, they're fine. What about yours?"

"Emancipation day is May fifteenth. That's when the twins graduate from college."

(151)

"Mary, shall we go to Ruzzi's? The food's good and Tony Ruzzi likes me. I send all of my juries there for dinner."

Mary Jackson laughs appreciatively. Then Barth guides her to Ruzzi's, a tiny red-bricked restaurant which is squeezed in between a Chinese laundry and a bakery. Barth is welcomed at the door by Tony Ruzzi, quite literally, with open arms. He and Mary Jackson are escorted to the table behind Ruzzi's front window. They will serve as Tony Ruzzi's featured attraction today. Bureaucratic royalty, like Judges Jackson and Barth, come to Ruzzi's, Tony Ruzzi is telling potential customers. Barth and Mary Jackson ignore the exploitation and order Beefeater martinis.

"You know, Mary, while I was waiting for you, I started thinking about that Parker homicide trial. You remember it, don't you?"

"You bet, I remember it. You know, Jim, I didn't want to try that case before you. You'd just come on the bench. I didn't know what kind of judge you were. But I did know some of those characters you'd represented. Very establishment and, for my money, crooked as hell."

"So who says they don't deserve good representation?"

"Well, I can tell you I was plenty worried. My client had been in jail for twenty-one months. Can you believe that, Jim? Twenty-one months. And he was innocent."

"You did all right with that one, Mary. Mr. Parker walked out of the courtroom a free man."

Barth indicates to a waiting Tony Ruzzi that they are prepared to order. "What looks good to you, Mary?" asks Barth.

"I'm going to have the chef's salad and coffee."

"What I have in mind for lunch," says Barth, "will cast considerable doubt on my credentials as a serious calorie counter. But I'm starved. Tony, how is the manicotti today?"

"Excellent, Judge," Ruzzi replies, smiling approvingly.

(152)

"Then I'll have manicotti with a side order of meatballs," Barth says quickly, as though the faster he says it, the less his stomach will notice the size of his order.

"Tell me about being a judge," Barth says, relieved to be changing the subject. "It's been six months for you, hasn't it?"

"It's been six long months, Jim. And that's part of the reason I suggested lunch. I need a little pep talk. I'd always thought, when I was a lawyer, that it would be great to be a judge. Well, I was wrong. All of my worst suspicions about judges are now confirmed. I've got cases up to here," says Mary Jackson, bringing her right hand up to her eyebrows. "And my colleagues on my left and right are doing nothing."

"So you've been introduced to our holy order," says Barth. "Is that all that's bothering you?"

"Not really," says Mary. "It's the job more than my colleagues. It's so depressing. Yesterday, I received a probation report that said the defendant had devoted his life to serious crime, beginning with a Murder One conviction fifteen years ago. Do you know what that murder conviction represented? The defendant was fourteen years old when he and another boy got into a fight with knives. In this state he couldn't even have been charged with murder at fourteen. But he was in another state and was convicted. Fourteen years old. Since he got out of jail, he's been convicted of possession of marijuana and vagrancy. That's his whole lifetime of serious crime."

Lunch arrives and Barth parts his first meatball. "Mary, you are learning fast," he says. "You now know that you can't believe probation reports. But you can't put all of the blame on the probation officers. Even the best of them can't do the job well. They have about the same amount of time to draw conclusions about each defendant as we do. In less than thirty minutes, probation officers, like judges, are supposed to draw deeply on the wisdom of criminology, psychology, and sociology to come up with a sound judgment. They can't do it and neither can we. When we've made a successful disposition, it usually means that we've used common sense, a modicum of legal knowledge, and had a bit of good old-fashioned luck."

"It makes me wonder," says Mary Jackson, shrugging her shoulders, "why I ever wanted to be a judge. My pay isn't that great. My colleagues, present company excepted, aren't that stimulating. And most of my time is spent making judgments that I know are superficial. As an attorney, at least I could dig into a case. I got to know my client as a person and a defendant. I could piece together the facts of the case for myself and I could present my case to the jury. I was involved. As a judge, I'm always aloof, not just in the sense of being on the bench above everybody else, but in the intellectual sense as well. I sit around and let the lawyers do the work. If they do a shabby job, there's not much I can do except overrule their objections and deny their motions. What I'm saying, I guess, is that I'm frustrated in my new job."

"You'll get over that feeling," says Barth. I think all judges feel frustrated at times, particularly those like yourself who come to the bench from a vigorous trial practice. But there are compensations. You do affect people, sometimes more than the attorneys. For example, take that fourteen-year-old you spoke of who the probation department reported was devoted to a lifetime of crime. As his attorney, even you probably couldn't have beaten the pot and vagrancy charges. But as a judge, you could look beyond the charges and save that fellow several years in prison. That's no mean achievement, whether you're grading yourself as an officer of the law or simply as a caring human being."

Barth stops speaking suddenly, almost embarrassed by the intensity with which he has expressed himself. He takes a final bite of manicotti and looks up, smiling. "I'm not saying you can always strike a blow for humanity in this job. Sometimes finding meaning in our role as judges becomes very complicated. Right now, I've got a black man on trial for rape. His record is as long as your arm. And I'd stake my pension that he's guilty as hell. But he's gambling that the victim, who is also black, won't be able to persuade a jury of eleven whites and one black of his guilt. And he may be right."

Talk of the Franklin trial reminds Barth that he is late for the afternoon session. He calls for the check. After paying the bill, he and Mary Jackson hurry back to their respective courtrooms.

2:18 P.M.

Mrs. Delores Harper takes the witness stand. She is an attractive woman of thirty-eight whose shapely figure is shown to good advantage in a snug white sweater and powder-blue skirt. Responding to Prosecutor Snowden's questions, Mrs. Harper tells the jury that she works as a cashier on the 3:30 to 11:30 shift at the Rivoli movie theater. She is married and has a twenty-year-old son, but currently lives with a boyfriend, Leroy Armstrong, in an apartment at 311 Grove Street.

On the evening of July 17, Mrs. Harper tells the jury, she left the theater at 11:30 and walked six blocks to the bus stop at the corner of Main and First Streets. As on other work nights, she expected to meet her boyfriend, Leroy Armstrong, and ride the bus home with him. That night, however, Armstrong did not show up. Thinking he must have been unavoidably delayed, Mrs. Harper decided to take the bus alone, anticipating that Armstrong would take the next bus twenty minutes later and meet her in the apartment. After she got off the bus, she walked to her apartment. As she unlocked the front door to her apartment building, "this guy grabbed me."

"Could you describe the man who grabbed you?" asks Snowden.

"He had mixed gray hair. He had blotches on his face. And he was ugly," she replies emphatically.

"Could you tell us what your attacker was wearing?" asks Snowden.

"I was so frightened I didn't notice. I don't know whether he was wearing a jacket or what. All that I know is that he was sweating and had these blotches." Delores Harper speaks forcefully, without fright or the hint of intimidation. As she describes her attacker, she looks directly at Willie Franklin. The defendant is unperturbed, listening to Mrs. Harper's story with all of the fascination of someone hearing a moderately interesting tale of someone else's mischief.

"Mrs. Harper, could you step down and demonstrate to the jury how you were grabbed?" asks Snowden.

Franklin's attorney, Martin Bowers, objects to the demonstration as calculated to inflame the jury and prejudice his client's defense.

"I'll allow it," says Barth.

Delores Harper walks directly to the front of the jury box and says, "Like this." She grabs Snowden's right arm and swings it around her neck. She puts his left arm on hers, behind her back in a hammer lock.

While Snowden holds the witness, he asks how Mrs. Harper could see her attacker.

"Oh, I could see him," she says as she jerks her head around and looks directly into Snowden's eyes. "He wanted me to see him."

"Had you ever seen him before?"

"No."

"Can you identify the man who attacked you?"

"I sure can. He's sitting right over there," she says, pointing to Willie Franklin. The defendant looks blankly at his accuser.

"Did the defendant say anything to you while you were in the entrance hall?" asks Snowden.

"He told me not to scream. He said not to fight him because it wouldn't do any good. He said, 'I'm going to fuck you.' The witness pauses, shuts her eyes, then repeats, "He said, 'I'm going to fuck you.' "

"What time was this Mrs. Harper?"

"A little after midnight, I think."

"So the defendant grabbed you at the entrance to your apartment about twelve fifteen. Then what did he do?"

"He forced me up the stairs. I tried to stop him, but he just kept pulling me up the stairs. As we were going up, he said again, 'You might as well come on because I'm going to have you anyway.' "

As Delores Harper describes the events leading to the rape, her voice is strong, giving the impression of rising anger. Willie Franklin listens impassively.

"After the defendant pushed you up the stairs and forced you to open your apartment door, what happened?"

"He asked me if my boyfriend was home."

"And what did you say?"

"I told him he might be."

"What did he say?"

"He just said that didn't matter."

"Then what happened, Mrs. Harper?"

"He pushed me into the bedroom and told me to take off my clothes."

"And what did you do?"

"I refused."

"And then what happened?" asks Snowden.

"Then he took them off. He took off my blouse and slacks. And then he ripped my panties and bra off," she says.

"Are these the panties and bra he ripped?" asks Snowden as he holds up bright red panties and a black brassiere that he has picked up from the counsel table. When the witness nods, Snowden offers the panties and bra into evidence. Bowers examines them briefly, then says he has no objection.

(157)

"What did the defendant do after he ripped off your panties and bra?"

"He told me to lie on the bed."

"And what did you do?"

"I didn't do anything."

"And what did he do?"

"He threw me onto the bed."

"Mrs. Harper, did Willie Franklin say anything to you?"

"Yes. He said I shouldn't fight him. It would be easier for both of us, he said, if I didn't fight him."

"What happened next, Mrs. Harper?"

"He forced himself inside me." Now the words rush out. "And he had a climax. That's for sure. I never, never will forget it." Mrs. Harper winces, as if in physical pain.

The witness testifies that after the attack, she saw Willie Franklin take a five-dollar bill out of her purse and a pillow and electric fan from her room. When he left, Mrs. Harper says that she ran out of her third-floor apartment, shouting that she had been raped. A few minutes later, Charles Mapes came up to the third floor and tried to calm her down.

"What time was this, Mrs. Harper?" asks Snowden.

"About quarter to one."

"What did you do then?"

"I didn't know what to do I was so upset. Charles said I should take a douche. So I took a douche."

"What time was that, Mrs. Harper?"

"It was about one o'clock, I think."

"And did you report the attack to the police?"

"Yes, I did. I called the next day after I had gone to the hospital for an examination."

"When did you next see your assailant, Willie Franklin?"

"Six days after the attack, I was shopping with my boyfriend, Leroy Armstrong, on Grove Street and I saw him. The same guy who had attacked me. I never will forget him as long as I live. Never."

"What did you do after you saw the defendant?"

"I didn't want to tell Leroy."

"Leroy Armstrong, your companion?"

"That's right. I didn't want to tell him because I was afraid there would be trouble. So I went to a phone booth and called the police. When the police came, he was still standing there. So I pointed to him."

"To Willie Franklin, the defendant?"

"Yes, that's right."

"What happened next?"

"The police put him in a squad car and drove away."

"I have no further questions."

Delores Harper should have made a favorable impression on the jury, Barth is thinking. The sweater and tight skirt suggest that the witness has not been living in a convent. But that's pretty clear from her background anyway. Her responses to Snowden's questions were direct and appeared to be candid. I think she came across as a sincere, law-abiding citizen who has been a victim of a serious crime. Mr. Snowden's biggest problem is that this jury may penalize Mrs. Harper for her life-style. Living with her boyfriend, the jurors may decide, makes her a loose woman. From there, it's just a short step to deciding that she picked up Mr. Franklin, or someone else that night. Afraid that her boyfriend would catch her, so the theory goes, she charged rape. I don't buy this theory and I don't think the jury will either. Particularly if the one black juror has his say. He should be able to educate the rest on the mores in such neighborhoods. And he can convince them that Delores Harper is a solid citizen, just as they are. She has a steady job. She has a grown child. She's no troublemaker. Now Mr. Franklin is something else again. At forty-eight, you would think the fires would have subsided. You never know.

Defense Attorney Martin Bowers rises for his cross-examination of Delores Harper. He gives the witness a perfunctory smile and then gets down to business.

(159)

"Mrs. Harper, did you have an argument with your boyfriend on July seventeenth?" asks Bowers. There is a coolness in his voice that undercuts his surface courteousness.

"No," the witness answers.

"Were you upset with him for any reason that night?"

"No."

"Well, you were upset when your boyfriend didn't meet you at the bus, weren't you?"

"A little. But not too much. I thought he would catch the next bus."

"You thought he would catch the next bus." Bowers pauses for a moment, cocks his right elbow, and puts his right hand to his chin, appearing deep in thought. "Mrs. Harper, when would that next bus have come?"

"The bus comes every twenty minutes."

"Every twenty minutes," Bowers repeats. "So you expected your boyfriend to be back at the apartment approximately twenty minutes after you. Is that right?"

"Well, that's what I thought."

"Mrs. Harper, when you got to the apartment and, you say, a man put his arm around your neck, did you yell for help?"

"No."

"Why not?"

"I was too scared."

"And when this man dragged you up the stairs, did you yell for help?"

"No."

"Why not?"

"I was afraid to."

"You are saying, then, that a man grabbed you around the neck, said he was going to rape you, dragged you up two flights of stairs, and you didn't yell for help. You didn't yell for help in your own apartment building, is that what you're saying, Mrs. Harper?"

Snowden is on his feet. "Objection, Your Honor. Mrs. Harper has already answered the question."

"Sustained," says Barth.

"I would also ask that the question be stricken from the record," says Snowden. "It was leading and in the form of a statement."

"Mr. Bowers," Barth says quietly, "please confine yourself to questions."

Bowers paces back and forth before the witness, his arms folded in front of him. "Now, Mrs. Harper, would it be fair to say that the man you say attacked you was agitated, worked up emotionally when he assaulted you?"

"Yes. Absolutely."

"Did your attacker unbutton your blouse?" asks Bowers.

"Yes."

"Without ripping it?"

"I suppose so."

"That's pretty cool behavior on the part of a frenzied attacker, wouldn't you say, Mrs. Harper?"

"Objection," shouts Snowden.

"Sustained."

Bowers strides to the prosecutor's table and picks up the panties that the prosecutor has introduced in evidence. He appears to examine them carefully. With his face in full view of the jury, Bowers frowns and looks troubled.

"You said, Mrs. Harper, that your attacker ripped these panties off. Is that correct?"

"Yes, he did."

"The only damage I see is two small tears in the lace," Bowers says.

"All I know is that the man ripped my panties off," says the witness firmly. "That's all I know."

"And the bra," says Bowers, holding the bra up for the jury to see. "It looks to me as if only a strap has been loosened."

"Objection," Snowden says. "The degree of damage to Mrs. Harper's undergarments is a question of fact for the jury to decide."

"Sustained."

"This is the bra that you said was ripped off you, is it not, Mrs. Harper?"

"That's right."

"Now after this attacker ripped your bra and panties off," Bowers says, his inflection suggesting disbelief, "how long were you in bed with him?"

"It was an eternity for me. I know that."

"Well, how long after he *ripped* your undergarments off did it take before you had intercourse?"

"I don't know," replies Delores Harper, her voice cracking for the first time. "After he got my legs apart, that's when he did it."

"Did you resist him?"

"I sure did. I tried to push him away. But he just kept on top of me."

"Did you slap him?"

"No."

"Why not?"

"I couldn't. He was on top of me."

"Did you scream?"

"No."

"Why not?"

"I was too frightened."

"Did you have a climax?"

"No, I did not."

"Did you put your arms around him?"

"No."

Bowers pauses a moment, then shifts his line of questions to the identification of Mrs. Harper's attacker. "Mrs. Harper, how would you describe your attacker?"

"He was dark-skinned and ugly."

"Nothing more?"

"All that I know is that that's the man there," she says, pointing to Franklin. "That's for sure."

"When you saw the man you say attacked you, on the street six days after the attack, did he look exactly the same as he had the night of the attack?"

"Yes, he did."

"Mrs. Harper, according to the police report, you told detectives that the man on the street wore a white patch on his face?"

"Yes, I did."

"You didn't mention that the man in your apartment had a patch. Did he?"

"No, he didn't. But it was the same man."

"So, the man on the street with the patch didn't look the same as the man in your bedroom six days before. Isn't that right?"

"It was the same man. I would know him anywhere, whether he wore a patch or not."

Bowers pauses a moment, then retreats to the defense table to refer to his notes. "Mrs. Harper, how long would you say it took from the time you boarded the bus at midtown until you met Charles Mapes in the apartment hallway after the incident?"

"I don't know. I guess about an hour and a half. But I wasn't looking at any watch. I was too scared."

"You testified earlier, I believe, that you expected your boyfriend, Leroy Armstrong, to take the next bus from midtown which, you said, would have come twenty minutes after yours. Is that correct?"

"That's right."

"Well, then, Mrs. Harper, where was Leroy Armstrong at twelve thirty-five, the approximate time he would have arrived in your apartment if he had taken the next bus?"

"I don't know," she replies.

"I have no further questions, Your Honor."

Somebody on that jury ought to be intelligent enough, thinks Barth as he walks back to his office, to see that Mr. Bowers can't make up his mind about which theory to pursue. Theory number one is that nothing happened in Delores Harper's apartment that night and she is framing the defendant. Theory number two is that Delores Harper had a spat with her boyfriend and was engaged in a pleasant interlude with Mr. Franklin. Theory number three is that there was a rape in Mrs. Harper's apartment but the attacker was not Willie Franklin.

Mr. Bowers can talk all day long about the prosecutor's duty to establish guilt beyond a reasonable doubt, but he still must be logical in his defense. And by confusing the jury with three conflicting theories of innocence, he is not helping himself. Did Delores Harper frame Willie Franklin? Unlikely. That jury has observed Delores Harper for several hours now. I don't think she strikes them as the devious type. The second approach, that Delores and Mr. Franklin were having a good time, possibly spurred by Delores's anger at her roommate, Leroy Armstrong, is okay. The trouble is that Mr. Bowers can't decide whether Willie Franklin was in that apartment with Delores Harper or not. If somebody else was in Delores's apartment, then Bowers can suggest a case of mistaken identity, theory number three. But what he should not suggest is that he has not made up his mind about which theory he wants to pursue.

4:53 p.m.

Delores Harper's testimony was completed earlier than I expected, Barth is thinking, as he eases into his big leather desk chair in his chambers. I still think that we can wrap up all of the testimony in the Franklin trial by tomorrow afternoon.

In the meantime, I can concentrate on my opinion in the Gilbert case.

He reaches for the Gilbert folder on his desk and pulls out a letter written in longhand on a single sheet of notebook paper: "Dear Judge Barth: Thank you for informing me that I can have a lawyer at the hearing in your court. I would prefer to represent myself. But as a last resort, I will take a lawyer because it is better than nothing. All that Judge Pearson had to do was keep the bargain he made for the five years and I would be more than satisfied. Why all this trouble? You are the people who made plea bargaining legal. Yours truly, Roger Gilbert #29108."

Should I believe Gilbert? asks Barth after rereading the letter Gilbert wrote to him three weeks ago. Here's a guy who's been a professional jewel thief most of his adult life. Still, he decides to take on a judge. Why? I'm sure he's been to the track. He can calculate odds and he's got to know it's one hell of a long shot.

And what about Gilbert's attorney, Whitney Barnes? He may come before Judge Pearson after this case is over. And he must know that Pearson is not going to take kindly to a lawyer who has publicly challenged his integrity. What's in it for Barnes? Maybe he gave Gilbert his word that he'd stick by him if Pearson reneged on his promise of a five-year term. Honor may yet live in this era of Watergate. Or maybe Barnes has been reading George Higgins and knows what happens when the mob is double-crossed.

Finally, there is Judge Randolph Pearson himself. Nobody has ever accused Randy Pearson of getting to the top of his profession by hard work and an incisive legal mind. No, Randy has always traded on his charm and native shrewdness. True, he got into a little trouble a few years ago with some get-rich-quick schemes, but that blew over. And Randy always worked hard and effectively for the Democrats, and that work got him his judgeship.

(165)

On the bench, Randy Pearson has continued his shrewd and charming ways. He's built a reputation as a liberal judge. Defense attorneys consider him one of the fairest judges on the bench, which means he'll give away the courthouse if nobody's looking. Not because Randy's been reading Marcuse and Eldridge Cleaver. No, Randy has found a happy merger between public humanitarianism and private self-interest: by getting pleas, even if they are far below what the defendants deserve, Randy Pearson saves the down-trodden a lot of jail time and himself a lot of courtroom time.

But with the Gilbert case, Randy Pearson had faced a problem. It had not been the kind of case he could have quickly dumped with a low plea. Too much publicity involved. Too much at stake in the DA's office. So Pearson had gone through the motions of a bona fide trial proceeding, beginning with the pre-trial motion to bar the admission of the stolen jewelry into evidence. Almost immediately, however, he must have realized that any ruling he could have made on the pre-trial motion would have meant later trouble. If he had ruled in favor of the defense, the DA's case would have been in shambles. Pearson probably could just see the headlines: PEARSON THROWS OUT KEY EVIDENCE; DA SAYS ENTIRE GILBERT CASE IN JEOPARDY. No, Randy Pearson would not have liked that. But what had been the alternative? If he had ruled in favor of the DA on the pre-trial motion, he ran a high risk of being reversed on appeal. The State Court of Appeals has been very careful to scrutinize the "reasonableness" of police searches and seizures of evidence, such as the jewelry found in Roger Gilbert's apartment.

Probably the more Randy Pearson thought about it, the more he had realized that the only solution was to get a plea before he had to decide that pre-trial motion to suppress the evidence at the trial. In his inimitable style, then, Pearson had begun to apply pressure on both sides to get his plea. The DA and defense attorney knew that Pearson's decision on the motion to suppress the DA's evidence would affect their strategy in selecting the jury. They also knew that the Code of Criminal Procedure forbids the selection of the jury before a ruling on the pre-trial motion. Pearson's contrary judicial interpretation of the code at my hearing had been for one purpose only: to protect himself on the public record. Pearson knows the law as well as Barnes and Rollins. And the law is that a judge must rule on a pre-trial suppression motion before the jury selection can begin. But when Barnes and Rollins had objected to Pearson's failure to rule on the pre-trial motion before initiating jury selection, Randy just smiled and took them to lunch.

Even with his pressure tactics, Pearson had not been able to get both sides to agree on a plea. So he invited Barnes into his robing room and made a commitment of his own to get things moving. If Barnes and his client, Roger Gilbert, agreed to a plea of attempted armed robbery, Pearson promised that Gilbert would be sentenced to no more than five years in prison. Barnes and Gilbert grabbed it.

But Pearson didn't let Assistant DA Rollins in on the promise. Why? He must have known, as everybody else around the courthouse does, that Rollins is politically a very ambitious young man. A guaranteed top of five years for a professional jewel thief who had pulled one of the slickest and most publicized heists in years just was not a promise that an ambitious young prosecutor would agree to. So Pearson told Rollins that the plea was attempted robbery with *no* promises. And Rollins agreed to it.

But something Randy Pearson had not counted on must have happened after he got his plea. My hunch is that the DA's office heard about the secret deal that Randy had worked out with Gilbert and Barnes. And somebody in the DA's office got on the phone and told Pearson if he followed through on his deal, the DA would indict *him*. Randy knows enough law to conclude that the statute of limitations had not run out on his old get-rich-quick schemes. If the DA had wanted to, he could have made things very uncomfortable for Randy Pearson. So Pearson told the DA's office that he had made no deal with Gilbert and that he could sentence him to fifteen years, which is what he did.

Randy had figured that Gilbert and Barnes would not take on a state criminal court judge, even if that judge had double-crossed them. But that was Pearson's critical miscalculation. When Randy pulled his double-cross, Gilbert screamed. He knew that Judge Randy Pearson had swindled him and he vowed not to let him get away with it without a fight.

Barth walks to the liquor cabinet, pours some Scotch into a glass, and returns to his desk. All of the pieces seem to fit together. Randy Pearson had been looking for the easiest way out of a progressively more complicated situation. He ordered jury selection without deciding the pre-trial motion. He knows that's wrong. He titillated each side with hints that he might rule against them on crucial points of law. He knows that's wrong, too. He courted attorneys on both sides, even treating them to lunch. Again, he knows that's wrong. And he promised the defendant five years and gave him fifteen. That is the ultimate outrage. Gilbert may be a no-good hood but he does have some rights. One of those rights is to be treated fairly in a court of law. And being double-crossed by Judge Randolph Pearson is not fair.

Barth stretches his arms high above his head. He feels satisfied that his basic conclusions on the Gilbert case are sound. He still has to put his opinion on paper, but that can wait until tomorrow morning. Randy Pearson will not, Barth reflects, receive the opinion with great enthusiasm. Well to hell with Randy Pearson. The hearing had not been for his benefit. And my courtroom is not the meeting place for the fraternal order of lazy, incompetent, and dishonest judges either. I just can't worry about what Randy Pearson and his cronies will do after they read my decision. Helen will do that. Helen! Barth takes a panicked look at his watch. Six o'clock.

I'd better get moving. Helen's probably downstairs now, wondering where I am. The first thing that she's going to ask is what I'm going to write in the Gilbert opinion. And I'll have to tell her. But if I tell her over a thick steak and baked potato, it might not worry her so much. And if that doesn't work, maybe a good movie. . . .

V
Friday

7:07 A.M.

Barth is depressed this morning. He sips his first cup of coffee and tries to analyze his mood. Could it be that movie Helen and I saw last night? Not likely. As a wiretapping and bugging expert, Harry Caul was not a character to inspire confidence in our advanced technological age. But, of course, that wasn't the point. Gene Hackman played the part superbly. In fact, I can't remember the last time I enjoyed a movie more.

Maybe it's the Gilbert opinion. Helen did raise some good points last night. Just because Randy Pearson does not perform his job in the same way as I do, isn't the best reason for me to condemn him. Aside from welching on a promise to Gilbert, Pearson's major error was to force a plea. So Pearson and I see our roles as judges differently. Does that mean that his brand of justice is inferior to mine?

After all, I could easily question every one of my own decisions. Should I have paroled Jesse Norwood, that fellow who

(173)

burned the curtains in his hotel room, knowing that he's had some mental problems? I don't know, but I had to make a choice anyway. What about Robert Alton, who makes his living, when he's out of prison, sticking up bars? He's unstable, uneducated, and unskilled. God knows, another fifteen years in state prison isn't going to do him any good. But the alternative is to let him out and wait until he really hurts somebody. And what should I do with John Harding, whom I have to sentence for armed robbery and the assault of Karen Petersen? Except for this conviction, Harding has no serious criminal record. And this conviction, I'm convinced, was the consequence of an impulsive act. Should Harding be put away for fifteen years with Robert Alton? The statute says that I can do that. But the statute doesn't tell me what benefit—to Harding or society—a fifteen-year prison term will have.

Randy Pearson and I don't have time to contemplate the perfect justice of the future. Our calendars are cluttered with the realities of today: the Norwoods and Altons and Hardings—and the Roger Gilberts. It's a depressing business. But somebody has to administer "justice," such as it is. And the public has the right to demand that we do it as fairly as the law will allow. It's not an easy job, so there's always the temptation to choke, mistaking caution for fairness, laziness for generosity. That's what happened to Randy Pearson.

He didn't start out intending to be unfair to Roger Gilbert. But he hadn't wanted to make the tough decisions either. So, eventually, he was unfair and, ultimately, dishonest. Maybe that's why the Gilbert case has given me such fits. Randy Pearson's conduct is a challenge to what I value in this imperfect system. If his performance can be condoned or ignored, then my values can be chucked out the window. And even admitting all of my middle-class, establishment foibles, I still believe that there is a lot about the way I think and act in my role as judge that is worth preserving.

Barth wants to dictate several letters this morning before going to court. The first concerns Judge Jack Gordon. Barth has heard that Gordon is being considered for nomination to the appellate court. The rumor alone, Barth has decided, is worth a letter to the Governor's mansion.

"Betsy, can you come in here and bring your pad, please?"

As soon as his secretary sits down, Barth begins dictation. "This is a letter to the Governor. 'My dear Governor: It was with a sense of horror that I heard that, as one of the proposed candidates for the state appellate court, Judge Jack Gordon's name has been put forward.

" 'While I recognize that there is an enormous range of opinion as to the capacity of judges, that is not the case with Judge Gordon. Since I am the assignment judge for Judge Gordon, I have had the misfortune of having to work with him on a day-to-day basis. From court clerks, court officers, court reporters, defense counsel, district attorneys, and jurors, I have never heard anyone speak a good word about the man. It would be a demoralizing blow to those concerned with even-handed justice if he should be elevated to the appellate court. Surely, there are intelligent, competent people who are qualified for the office. Very truly yours.' "

The next letter is addressed to Bobby Mitchell at the state penitentiary. Barth had sentenced Mitchell to fifteen years for armed robbery a month ago. Since then, Mitchell has written several letters to Barth from prison, complaining that he was not getting credit for jail time that he had served before he was sentenced. He turned to Barth, Mitchell had written, because he couldn't think of anyone else who might help him.

Barth liked his spirit and was flattered that Mitchell would turn to the person who was, at least in part, responsible for his present predicament. Two weeks ago, Barth had made copies of Mitchell's letters and sent them, with his covering letter asking for an accounting, to the Commissioner of Corrections. Then he put Melvin on the case. Melvin, Barth knew, would simply badger and harass the Department of Corrections until somebody there would take an interest in the case just to get rid of him. And it had worked. Earlier this week, Barth had received a letter from the Department of Corrections informing him that Bobby Mitchell had not been credited with 241 days of jail time that he had coming to him.

" 'Dear Mr. Mitchell: I am enclosing a copy of a letter I have received from the Department of Corrections crediting you with 241 days of jail time. If this is not correct, please let me know. Otherwise, I will consider the matter settled. Very truly yours . . . '

"Just a few more minutes, Betsy. I want to get one more letter off." The congressman from Barth's district has taken an unpopular stand on the pocketbook issue of taxes recently and Barth has read that many of his constituents are complaining. " 'Dear Congressman: In keeping with the code of judicial ethics, I won't take a position on public issues. But I assume you have two piles of letters responding to your recent vote on the tax bill. Put this in the smaller pile. Yours truly . . . ' "

9:11 A.M.

Barth arrives in his courtroom a few minutes earlier than usual. Since his courtroom does not open officially for business until 9:30, he feels a little guilty about taking time that he could use to begin drafting his Gilbert opinion. But he soon forgets the Gilbert opinion and is content to sit at the bench, taking no pleas, sentencing no defendants, not even reading the morning newspaper. The quiet of the courtroom is special to Barth; he will be bombarded soon enough with demands on his professional time. But as he watches lawyers, court officers, and relatives of defendants slowly drift in, he reminds himself that the courtroom is for people with problems. Sustained periods of quiet are for professors of jurisprudence, but not for state criminal court judges.

"Judge," says George Giles, handing Barth a gray folder, "here's a reduced bail application for Robert Lindsay."

Barth opens the folder and scans Lindsay's record. He is currently charged with the armed robbery of a clothing store, has two prior felony convictions and six misdemeanors. He has asked for a bail reduction on the basis of an endorsement letter from the director of Sunshine House Drug Rehabilitation Center and verification from the probation department that he has a family in the city and a girlfriend he intends to marry.

"George, get Lindsay up here. We'll take care of his application and then go right into the Franklin trial."

A few minutes later, Lindsay, an imposingly tall man, stalks to the defense table. He is dressed in gray trousers and purple turtleneck shirt and sports a striking handlebar mustache.

"Your Honor," says Lindsay's attorney, a mild-mannered man named Watson, "we believe reasonable bail should be set for this defendant. His mother and girlfriend are here. So is the director of Sunshine House, who believes, as you know from his letter, that Mr. Lindsay would be an excellent candidate for his drug rehabilitation program."

"That does not speak well for the program's screening process," Barth says sarcastically. "This defendant has two prior felony convictions and six misdemeanors. The present charge is robbery at gun point. If I were to lower bail and the defendant returned to this court, you, counsel, would have the defense that your client is mentally unbalanced. The secured bond remains at ten thousand dollars."

"May I say something, Your Honor?" Lindsay asks.

Barth nods.

(177)

"I wasn't doing anything when I was arrested. I was not identified at the line-up. I just don't understand it. What kind of justice do we have here? I tell you, Judge, I'm not guilty."

"That's why we are going to give you a trial," Barth says. "Twelve of your peers will then decide if they believe your story."

"May I at least see my family, who are here in court this morning?" asks Lindsay belligerently. "That's the least you can do for me, since you haven't done anything else."

"Remand the defendant," says Barth.

As court officers Lorenzo and Mitchell start to lead Lindsay back to jail, the defendant shouts angrily at Barth, "For the record, I'd like to say you're a no-good motherfucker."

Barth stares straight at Lindsay, trying very hard to appear unperturbed by his outburst. But inside, he is second-guessing himself. *Maybe I should have let him see his family. It's a small enough request. But there is something in Lindsay's attitude —that reduced bail and a visit with his family are his rights—that put me off. He has rights in this courtroom—to counsel and to a fair trial. But Mr. Lindsay does not seem to distinguish between his legal rights and his personal demands. That is not a constructive attitude for him or anybody else to take in my courtroom.*

"George, let's move with the Franklin trial," says Barth. "Get Franklin up here and bring in the jury."

While he is waiting, Barth reflects on the trial: *The prosecution's star witness, Delores Harper, impressed me yesterday. Her description of the rape was credible and her identification of Willie Franklin as her attacker was solid. Franklin's attorney, Martin Bowers, suggested in his cross-examination that Delores Harper had not tried to repel her attacker, hinting that it was not a forced attack and, therefore, not rape. Bowers also tried to get Mrs. Harper to admit that she was not sure that her* attacker was Willie Franklin. Fair enough cross-examination, but I don't think he scored many points with the jury. He didn't with me.

The defendant and the jurors settle into their seats and Giles announces that the trial of "The People versus Willie Franklin" is in session. Prosecutor Tom Snowden calls to the stand Charles Mapes, a slight man with small, elegant features. Mapes is wearing a dazzling burnt-orange jumpsuit with a menacing cat embroidered in bold yellow thread on the back. In a high-pitched voice, Mapes identifies himself as a furniture refinisher, husband, father of two children, and downstairs neighbor of Delores Harper.

"Mr. Mapes, could you tell the jury where you were on the night of July seventeenth?" asks Snowden.

"Yes, I was in my apartment."

"And did you hear anything unusual that evening?"

"Yes."

"Tell the jury what you heard, Mr. Mapes."

"Sometime after midnight, I guess about twelve forty-five, I heard screams."

"Where were the screams coming from?"

"Above me. On the third floor."

"What did you do after you heard the screams?"

"I came out of my apartment to see what was wrong."

"And what did you see?"

"The first thing I saw was Racket coming down the stairs with a pillow and fan."

"Who is Racket, Mr. Mapes?"

"I don't know the man's real name but he's a man I see around the neighborhood and he's called Racket."

"Do you see the man you refer to as Racket in this courtroom, Mr. Mapes?"

"Yes, that's him," replies the witness, pointing to Willie Franklin.

"Now, Mr. Mapes, at approximately twelve forty-five A.M., when you saw the defendant coming down the stairs of your apartment building with a pillow and fan, did you say anything to him?"

"Yes. I asked what he was doing."

"And what did he say?"

"He said he'd been with Delores."

"Delores Harper?"

"Yes."

"Go on, Mr. Mapes."

"He said he'd met her in a bar and they'd had a couple of drinks."

"And what did you say?"

"I asked him why he was carrying a pillow and fan."

"What did Willie Franklin say?"

"He didn't say anything. He dropped the fan and pillow and left."

"Did he seem in a hurry at the time?"

"He sure did. He ran down the stairs and out the door."

"And what did you do, Mr. Mapes?"

"Well, about that time Delores came down from the third floor screaming. At first I couldn't understand what she was saying. She was hysterical. I finally calmed her down so I could understand her."

"And what did she say?"

"She told me she'd been raped."

"And what did you do?"

"I just tried to help her. I brought her into my apartment. My wife helped her take a douche."

"Your witness, Mr. Bowers," says Snowden.

Bowers rises slowly from his chair, walks to the front of the jury box, and stands absolutely still for a moment as if reciting a silent prayer. Then he turns to the witness.

"Mr. Mapes, is Mrs. Harper a friend of yours?"

"Yes, sir."

"As a friend, you would help her if she were in trouble, wouldn't you?"

"Yes, I would."

"Now you said that shortly after midnight on July seventeenth you saw a man named Racket come down the stairs after you heard screams. Is that right?"

"Yes."

"And he spoke to you?"

"Yes."

"What did he say, Mr. Mapes?"

"He said that he had met Delores at a bar and they had a couple of drinks."

"That's Delores Harper?"

"That's right."

"After you heard the screams from the third floor, did you try to hold this man?"

"No."

"Did you call the police?"

"No."

"Why not, Mr. Mapes?"

"I was busy helping Delores."

"I have no further questions, Your Honor," says Bowers.

As Mapes leaves the courtroom, Barth reflects on his testimony: Mr. Mapes offered one crucial piece of testimony for the prosecution. He identified Franklin and placed him at the scene on the night Delores Harper says she was raped. What's more, Mapes said that Franklin is known in the neighborhood, so he could hardly have confused the defendant with someone else. There goes Mr. Bowers's theory of mistaken identity. Another thing Mapes did. He gave verisimilitude to the prosecution's burglary and petty larceny charges. He saw Franklin coming down the stairs with a pillow and fan. Mapes's testimony creates problems for Mr. Bowers's theory

(181)

that Franklin and Mrs. Harper were upstairs having a nice time. A man who has consummated a happy affair one minute would not be likely to rush out the next with a pillow and fan, leaving his paramour screaming in the background. Bowers tried to make something of the fact that Mapes didn't stop Willie Franklin after he heard Delores yelling hysterically. But the jurors have seen Willie Franklin and they've seen Charles Mapes. Mr. Mapes may be a good friend of Delores's but, at five feet eight or nine, he would have been very ill advised to have started a fight with big Willie.

Snowden's next witness is Dr. Milton Simkins, the doctor who examined Delores Harper the day after she said she was raped. In brief, efficient sentences, Simkins testifies that Mrs. Harper's uterus was tender and that that tenderness could have been caused by rape.

On cross-examination, Defense Attorney Bowers asks, "Could that tenderness have been the result, Doctor Simkins, of voluntary intercourse?"

"Yes, possibly," Simkins replies.

"Doctor Simkins, in your examination of Mrs. Harper, did you discover any external injuries to Mrs. Harper?"

"No, sir."

"Did you find any evidence of sperm on Delores Harper's body when she was at the hospital?"

"No, sir."

Bowers says that he has no more questions. Just as Dr. Simkins is about to leave, Barth motions him to remain seated.

"Doctor Simkins," asks Barth, "if there were a twelve-hour delay between an attack and an examination, and the victim took a douche in between, is it likely that sperm would be found on the body?"

"No, Your Honor."

"Thank you, Doctor Simkins."

The next witness, Detective William Farrell, identifies himself as one of the policemen who met Delores Harper on Grove Street the day she pointed out Willie Franklin as her attacker. Farrell says that he and his partner arrested Franklin and took him to the police station. Farrell later interviewed Charles Mapes to verify Mrs. Harper's story. Snowden questions Detective Farrell about the arrest and investigation for only ten minutes; both prosecutor and witness appear bored by the exchange.

But Defense Attorney Bowers is not bored. And when it is Bowers's turn to cross-examine, he stands flat-footed only two feet away from the witness and begins to ask tough questions:

"Detective Farrell, what was the basis for your arrest of Willie Franklin?"

"After we got the call from Mrs. Harper, she pointed him out as the man who had raped her on the night of July seventeenth."

"Did you have any other reason to arrest the defendant?"

"No, sir, not at that time."

"So you arrested Willie Franklin and charged him with burglary, petty larceny, and rape in the first degree because one person picked him out of a crowd, six days after the alleged incident and said, 'That's the man'?"

"Objection," says Snowden. "The question is leading."

"Sustained."

"You arrested the defendant solely on the basis of Delores Harper's identification, six days after the crime had been reported. Is that correct?"

"Yes, sir."

"And did you follow up the arrest with an investigation?"

"Yes, sir."

"And what did that investigation consist of, Detective Farrell?"

"I interviewed Mrs. Harper and Mr. Mapes, her neighbor, in their apartment building."

"When did those interviews take place?"

(183)

"May I look at my notebook?"

"Certainly."

Farrell opens a little black notebook and reads for a moment. "It was August twenty-first," he says.

"You are telling us that you waited a full month after you arrested Willie Franklin before you investigated the case?" asks Bowers incredulously.

"Yes, sir. We had a considerable backlog, and that was the soonest that I could get to it."

Bowers focuses on the substance of Farrell's interviews for several minutes, searching for inconsistencies with the testimony of Delores Harper and Charles Mapes. He discovers none. He returns to his attack on Detective Farrell's investigation.

"Detective Farrell, have you reviewed the physical evidence in this case?"

"Yes, sir. I've examined Mrs. Harper's undergarments."

"When did you examine them?"

"They were brought down to the station yesterday."

"You did not see these undergarments until yesterday?" asks Bowers, raising his voice and eyebrows simultaneously.

"That's correct."

"I have no further questions."

Bowers asks Barth to excuse the jury so that he can introduce a motion to dismiss one of the charges against Franklin. Barth informs the jurors that they may take a short recess.

"Your Honor," says Bowers, after the jury has left, "I move to dismiss the charge of rape in the first degree. The prosecution has not satisfied the statutory requirement of proof for rape." To support his position, Bowers cites a two-year-old decision in which a rape charge was dismissed because, Bowers contends, there was no evidence corroborating the victim's testimony.

(184)

"I think you will find, Mr. Bowers," replies Barth, "that a full reading of the case you cite suggests that proof of forcible rape is a question of fact for the jury to determine."

"But, Your Honor," says Bowers, "the victim's testimony alone is not enough. There still must be corroborative evidence before the jury can decide the issue."

"What's the matter with Mr. Mapes?" asks Barth.

"Mr. Mapes did not testify that he saw any signs of force," Bowers responds.

Tom Snowden joins the argument. "Your Honor, I don't think there's any question that we've introduced evidence of physical force. In addition to Mrs. Harper's testimony, we have the testimony of Mr. Mapes, who observed Mrs. Harper immediately after the attack. We also have the torn undergarments of the complainant. It is now a matter for the jury to decide."

"Those undergarments were hardly damaged at all," Bowers argues. "They don't establish a *prima facie* case for the People."

"It is for the jury to determine the extent of resistance necessary to satisfy the statutory requirement of rape," says Barth. "The question of proof of forcible rape is a jury question. The motion of the defendant is denied. Anything else, Mr. Bowers?"

"No, Your Honor."

"Let's take a ten-minute break. Then you can put on your witnesses, Mr. Bowers."

"Your honor, the defense will call no witnesses."

So I was right, Barth reflects. Bowers is not putting Willie Franklin on the stand. He knows that forcible rape is difficult to prove and he doesn't think Snowden has done it. Bowers is not going to jeopardize his chances by putting Willie Franklin on the stand and letting Snowden take pot shots at him.

"You'll begin your summation in ten minutes, Mr. Bowers," says Barth.

"My purpose in this summation," says Bowers in an easy, conversational tone, "is to serve as a thirteenth juror. I want to explain the defense's point of view as if my client and I were in the jury room with you.

"Let me begin by saying that we consider rape a serious crime. There's no doubt about that. But it is your job to determine, first, if a rape in fact, took place. Secondly, if a rape did take place, was it Mr. Franklin who committed it? The judge will tell you later that the law of rape requires a finding that there be sexual intercourse and that that intercourse must be by force. If you do not find those two elements, sexual intercourse and force, you must find the defendant not guilty of rape.

"Now let's examine the evidence. First of all, was there intercourse? What is the evidence? You heard Doctor Simpkins testify that there was no semen on Mrs. Harper's body when he examined her. Nor was there semen on her clothing." Bowers pauses. "But Mrs. Harper says there was intercourse. So what you really have is her word, her word alone.

"You also have Mrs. Harper's word that the intercourse was by force. Of course, she has to say it was by force or there is no crime. Can you believe her? Let's examine the evidence. Mrs. Harper told you that her attacker ripped off her under-garments. . . ."

Bowers walks over to the prosecutor's table and picks up the red panties that Delores Harper has said that she was wearing when she was attacked. "I see two small tears in the lace, and that's it," says Bowers. "Is this the work of a rapist?" asks Bowers, casually holding up the panties as though they are fresh Kleenex. "I don't think so. Since we know from Detective Farrell's testimony that these pants weren't brought down to the police station until yesterday, that kind of damage could have resulted from routine wear and tear. It is not, I think you'll agree, the kind of damage one commonly associates with a vicious attack."

Bowers holds up the complainant's bra. "All that I see is a loosened strap," he says, carelessly dropping the bra on the prosecutor's table. "And we are supposed to believe that this was the clothing *ripped* from the complainant's body.

"If this was such a brutal attack, why weren't there any marks on the complainant? The medical report says there was not a single mark. Not a bruise. Not a scratch. If this was such a brutal attack, why weren't there any? And why, if this was such a vicious attack, did Mrs. Harper's attacker, by her own account, stop and unbutton her blouse, button by button. Is that the behavior of a rapist?

"There was not one whimper from Mrs. Harper when, by her account, she was dragged up two flights of stairs. Why didn't she resist or scream? This happened in her own apartment building, where, presumably, she had friends. Not a yell, not a whimper. And when, by Mrs. Harper's account, the attack took place, still no yelling, no resistance. Doesn't that seem remarkable to you? It does to me.

"Mrs. Harper says she was upset. But she waited more than twelve hours before going to the hospital to get examined. That's a long time. Is that the behavior one would expect of someone who has been raped? I don't think so.

"If this was such a serious crime, how do you explain the behavior of Detective Farrell? You heard him this morning. He didn't talk to anyone for a month after he reported the crime. Is this the work of a policeman who believes a violent rape has been committed? I don't think so. I think this policeman, who has been on the city force for many years, sized up the situation quickly. It was no attack and he knew it. So he went through the motions of an investigation when he had the time.

(187)

"Did Detective Farrell really think it was a violent rape or did he think Mrs. Harper picked someone up after an argument with her boyfriend, and later regretted it? Whatever Detective Farrell thought, he didn't think it was important to interview Mrs. Harper and Charles Mapes in the apartment building until a month after the incident. And he didn't think it was important enough to inspect the physical evidence until yesterday.

"It all makes you wonder. Was it a rape or a pickup? Was the man in Delores Harper's apartment there against her wishes? What prevents Delores Harper or anyone else from crying rape when they're in an embarrassing situation? Nothing. And what about the burglary and petty larceny charges? Preposterous. How could there possibly have been a burglary if the man in Mrs. Harper's apartment did not break in? If there was a man in Delores Harper's apartment that night, I submit he was invited. And why was he invited? He was invited there because Delores Harper had had a fight with her boyfriend. He had stood her up, or so she apparently thought.

"If her boyfriend had taken the next bus, as Mrs. Harper said he would, he would have been home twenty minutes after her. But he wasn't. So what did Mrs. Harper do? She found another friend. Even Charles Mapes, who testified for the prosecution, admitted that the man who came down the stairs that night said that he met Mrs. Harper in a bar and had a couple of drinks."

Bowers pauses a moment and searches the faces of the twelve jurors. "Ladies and gentlemen, if the facts in this case lead to two conclusions, you must take the one most favorable to Mr. Franklin. That is the law. I suggest in this case that the facts lead to many conclusions. One conclusion, and the one that I think the facts before you suggest, is that there was no rape in Delores Harper's apartment on the night of July seventeenth. A seduction, perhaps, but not a rape.

"I would suggest further that the facts presented do not show

(188)

that the man in Mrs. Harper's apartment was Mr. Franklin. Mrs. Harper testified that the man had a 'face I'll never forget.' Why, then, couldn't she describe the man in her apartment beyond a description of 'ugly and dark-skinned'? That's hardly a description of someone 'I'll never forget.' Who else testified? Charles Mapes. But you heard Mr. Mapes say he was a good friend of Mrs. Harper and would do anything to help if he could. As a friend, Mr. Mapes may have been stretching the truth. And in stretching the truth, Willie Franklin has been charged with rape. The facts, ladies and gentlemen, just don't show that Mr. Franklin has done such a thing.

"All that I ask is that you weigh all of the evidence and that you be sure, not to a mathematical certainty, but to a moral certainty and beyond a reasonable doubt, that Mr. Franklin is guilty. I submit that you can't do that. Based on the evidence presented in this case, you cannot possibly find my client guilty beyond a reasonable doubt.

"Thank you," Bowers says.

He sits down next to Willie Franklin and looks to his client for approval of his closing remarks. But Franklin gives no indication of approval or disapproval. He continues to chew gum and maintain a cool, impassive demeanor. Neither his facial expression nor the steady rhythm of his gum-chewing changes as Tom Snowden rises for his summation.

With a crisp, businesslike delivery, Snowden tells the jury that "a trial is nothing more than a formal search for truth under the rules of evidence. The purpose of the summation, ladies and gentlemen, is to help you evaluate the evidence with arguments that are based on reason and logic.

"There is only one issue in this case. Did the defendant, Willie Franklin, force Mrs. Delores Harper into her apartment, rape her, and take property from her? That's the issue. Don't lose sight of the bouncing ball. Don't be confused by all the speculative arguments of Mr. Bowers.

"You, ladies and gentlemen of the jury, must evaluate the

credibility of the witnesses in order to arrive at your verdict. First, there is the complainant, Mrs. Delores Harper. Mrs. Harper is married and has a grown child. She lives with her boyfriend. She is not a virgin and does not claim to be. But she is telling the truth. She has no reason to lie.

"Now let's review the facts. Mrs. Harper has testified that when she returned to her apartment, the man she has identified as Mr. Franklin grabbed her around the neck and said, 'I'm going to fuck you.' Mr. Bowers has made a big point of the fact that Mrs. Harper did not scream when she was grabbed. If someone had a stranglehold around your neck, I ask you, would you scream?

"After Willie Franklin dragged her up the stairs, he asked, 'Is your boyfriend home?' That's very important. How does Willie Franklin know that she has a boyfriend? He knows because he's observed Mrs. Harper and her boyfriend in the neighborhood. Mrs. Harper answers, 'My boyfriend may be home.' And then Willie Franklin says, 'It doesn't matter.' "

Snowden returns to his counsel table and lifts Mrs. Harper's red panties and bra. "Mr. Bowers would have us believe that this damage was the result of a few months ordinary wear and tear." Snowden holds up first the panties, then the bra, turning them to expose the damage to the garments. "I don't think so," he says. "Do you?

"You might ask, if Mrs. Harper was attacked and ran out of her apartment screaming, why didn't more people come out to help her? You've read stories of how people don't like to get involved in difficult situations. It's not unusual. But one person did want to get involved here. Charles Mapes. When he heard Mrs. Harper's scream, Charles Mapes came running out of his apartment. And what did he see? He saw Willie Franklin running down the stairs with a fan and a pillow in his hands.

" 'Hey, Racket, what are you doing?' asked Mr. Mapes. Franklin replied, 'I met Delores Harper in a bar and we had a couple of drinks.' But when Mapes asked him about the fan and the pillow, Franklin dropped them and ran out of the building. Think about that. If Willie Franklin had been in Mrs. Harper's apartment at her invitation, why would he be carrying a fan and a pillow out of her apartment? And why would he run down the stairs when Charles Mapes began asking questions? That doesn't make sense.

"Mr. Bowers has been critical of Mrs. Harper's description of the defendant. Remember, she was attacked. She was frightened. Under those circumstances, who could remember every detail of an attacker? Mrs. Harper is not a machine. She's a human being like you and me. Still, she told police that her attacker was male, black, ugly, and had blotches on the left side of his face. That description," says Snowden pointing at Willie Franklin, "fits the defendant perfectly.

"Mrs. Harper has testified that she was raped in her apartment on the night of July seventeenth and is certain that Willie Franklin was her attacker. Is there anything to support her testimony? Of course, there is. We have the torn underwear. And we have the testimony of Charles Mapes of what happened after the attack. Mr. Mapes described Mrs. Harper as coming down the stairs screaming. She was hysterical, he said. He also said that he saw Willie Franklin only moments before Mrs. Harper came out of her apartment screaming. Mr. Mapes even referred to Franklin by his street name. Racket. That's no mistaken identity.

"What defense have you heard? Mr. Bowers offered three theories, really, but never quite decided which he wanted you to believe. The first was conspiracy. Everybody's lying. Willie Franklin's been framed. Does that make sense? Does it really make sense for Delores Harper to come down here and subject herself to an embarrassing cross-examination and the charge that she is a loose woman? I don't think so. "You heard Doctor Simkins testify that Mrs. Harper's uterus was tender, which, he said, could have resulted from *forcible* intercourse. He also said that it was unlikely that the tenderness could have resulted from voluntary intercourse. Did he have a reason to lie? Of course not. Charles Mapes said he heard Delores Harper screaming and that he saw Willie Franklin, the man he knew as Racket, come down the stairs with a fan and a pillow. Would Mr. Mapes perjure himself just because he is a friend of Mrs. Harper's? You also heard Detective Farrell say that he saw Delores Harper point out Willie Franklin as her attacker. I ask you: Does this sound like a putup job? The answer has to be 'no.'

"Mr. Bowers's second theory is that Willie Franklin was, indeed, in Delores Harper's apartment on the night of July seventeenth but that he was there at Mrs. Harper's invitation. If that were so, Mrs. Harper would not have been screaming hysterically about being raped after bidding good-bye to an invited guest. And Willie Franklin, if he had been invited, would not have been leaving in such a hurry, with Mrs. Harper's pillow and fan in his arms. Finally, there would have been no ripped undergarments if this had been just a friendly interlude.

"Mr. Bowers's final theory is that this was all a case of mistaken identity. Mrs. Harper was attacked, but Willie Franklin wasn't the attacker. But, remember, both Mrs. Harper and Charles Mapes described Willie Franklin to a T. Mr. Mapes even knew Willie Franklin's street name. Racket. That's no case of mistaken identity.

"Ladies and gentlemen, beware the word-magician. Deal with the facts, not Mr. Bowers's fantasies and speculations. Use your common sense. When you do, I think you'll realize that you can draw only one conclusion from the evidence. And that is that Willie Franklin is guilty, beyond a shadow of a doubt, of the crimes of burglary, petty larceny, and rape in the first degree. Thank you."

(192)

Pretty good job, Mr. Snowden, Barth reflects, as he watches the prosecutor return to his chair with the same brisk efficiency that he has maintained throughout the trial. Snowden did what he was supposed to do. He gave an interpretation of the crime to dispel the doubts raised by the defense and he offered a plausible explanation to support his own theory.

Mr. Bowers did all right, too. He finally told the jury which theory he wanted it to believe: that there was no rape in Delores Harper's apartment. But even if the jury doesn't believe that, it does not have enough evidence to prove that the attacker was Willie Franklin. He might have done it a little more forcefully, though. My position, Bowers could have said, is that Willie Franklin was not in Delores Harper's apartment. But this woman says he was. Even assuming her story to be true, an assumption you should not make, Willie Franklin could not be guilty of the crimes he is charged with. If he was in Mrs. Harper's apartment, the evidence indicates he was there with her consent. If Bowers had made that argument more forcefully, he could have made a virtue out of his indecisiveness during the trial.

Well, Snowden and Bowers have certainly provided the jury with ample material for a provocative Friday afternoon discussion. Once they get lunch and my jury instructions out of the way, they'll be free to go to it.

1:22 P.M.

Barth picks up a tuna fish sandwich and cup of cottage cheese from the basement vending machine and heads for his office. He loathes vending machine lunches but he wants to get started on his Gilbert opinion. When Barth opens the door to his office, he is greeted by Melvin Rich, who is waving an early edition of the afternoon newspaper.

"Judge," says Melvin excitedly, "have you seen the paper?"

"No," replies Barth. "Should I have?"

"It's about that fellow you paroled yesterday. Jesse Norwood. You know, the guy who burned the curtains in his hotel room. Here he is on page three." Melvin hands Barth the paper: MAN, 21, IS KILLED AFTER ARGUMENT.

Barth's eyes drop down to the story.

A 21-year-old man was stabbed to death early this morning during an argument in a men's room at the city bus terminal. The police identified the victim as Robert Monroe Byrd, Jr., and said his body was found by a porter shortly after one A.M. in a lower-level men's room.

According to the police, an argument in the men's room led to the stabbing, but the cause of the dispute was not known. Police arrested Jesse Norwood, 27, as a suspect in the stabbing. Norwood, who lives in the Main Hotel, 460 West Main St., was seized by police outside the bus terminal shortly after Byrd's body was discovered. Police said the suspect, who had a seven-inch hunting knife in his possession, had admitted having an argument with Mr. Byrd in the terminal restroom.

Barth hands the newspaper back to Melvin without comment. Melvin shakes his head. "You never know, do you, Judge? Norwood seemed okay when he was in court yesterday. He made a good impression. A little nervous but very articulate. I would never have thought he would do something like this."

"What makes you think he did it, Melvin?" asks Barth irritably. "This is just a newspaper article. He's a suspect and must be presumed innocent, under our criminal justice system, until proven guilty beyond a reasonable doubt."

Melvin gives Barth a you've-got-to-be-kidding look. Barth ignores it and walks into his chambers. Actually, Barth is as surprised as Melvin. Well, so much for Mr. Norwood, he is thinking. I gambled and lost. Norwood was evidently a very poor risk. But could I have known that when I let him out?

Barth opens his lower-right-hand desk drawer and takes out the Norwood file. Naval veteran with an honorable discharge. That's certainly a plus. He's been hospitalized for mental disturbances. He hears voices and thinks people are after him. That's a minus. But he hasn't been in an institution for five years, and here's a psychiatric report, dated March 4, 1973, that says that Norwood is competent to stand trial.

Norwood had been in jail for four and a half months for setting fire to a curtain in his apartment. That's a misdemeanor in anybody's book. Four and a half months for burning a curtain is enough jail time. I thought so when Norwood was in court yesterday and I still think so. But there are those who'll say that if it hadn't been for Judge Barth's leniency, Mr. Robert Monroe Byrd, Jr., would be alive today. If I start thinking that way, I'll put 'em all in jail. The good risks and the bad. All of 'em. Then nobody can say anything. But if I do that, I'm choking. I'm not doing my job. And that's not going to happen.

2:14 P.M.

As the Franklin jury files into the courtroom for Barth's instructions, Barth studies each juror with the intensity of a professional scout grading college football prospects. First, the insurance executive who is the foreman. Has he made up his mind about Willie Franklin? If so, will he be able to win the other jurors to his view or will he relinquish control to a more forceful juror? Has Edna Morgan, department store clerk, reacted negatively to Delores Harper's life-style? If so, will that reaction determine how she will vote on Franklin? Most important, will the one black juror, interior designer Russell

Sones, stand up for Delores Harper in that jury room? Will he give the white jurors a cram course on life and risks in the black ghetto or will he simply drift to the majority position, whatever that might be?

"The first count of the indictment against the defendant, Willie Franklin, is burglary in the second degree," Barth tells the jury. "Burglary in the second degree is committed when a defendant has entered and remained unlawfully in a dwelling at night for the purpose of committing the crime of larceny. All elements of the crime, I remind you, ladies and gentlemen, must be established beyond the reasonable doubt. The second count of the indictment against the defendant, Willie Franklin, is petty larceny. The crime of petty larceny is committed when there is the stealing of property, that is, wrongfully taking or withholding property from its owner."

Finally, Barth explains the charge to which attorneys Martin Bowers and Tom Snowden have devoted most of their trial argument. "The third count of the indictment is rape in the first degree. To be found guilty of rape, the defendant must be shown to have engaged in sexual intercourse with the complainant by forcible compulsion. The legal definition of forcible compulsion is physical force that overcomes earnest resistance, or the threat of physical force, real or implied, that places the victim in danger of death."

Barth carefully makes the transition from the basic elements of the crime of rape to the evidentiary issue raised by Bowers's earlier motion to dismiss the charge. "The defendant cannot be convicted of the crime of rape in the first degree on the basis of the victim's testimony alone. There must be corroborating evidence. Obviously, ladies and gentlemen, such crimes aren't usually committed in the presence of many people. The victim's testimony must be considered. The statute's requirement that there be corroboration does not mean that corroborative testimony must be conclusive. It is for you, the jury, to decide the factual issue of guilt or innocence on the basis of all of the testimony you have heard as well as the physical evidence that has been presented." Before sending the jury to the conference room, Barth warns that "there is no formula for conducting your deliberations. You should reach a verdict, by whatever means, that is consistent with your concept of fairness."

And what, Barth asks himself as he watches the last juror leave the courtroom, will that "concept of fairness" be? That Willie Franklin is guilty as charged and should spend X number of years in prison as punishment? That Willie Frankin is guilty but that the prosecution has not proved his guilt beyond a reasonable doubt and, therefore, Franklin is "not guilty" under the law? That Willie Franklin is guilty but the jury of eleven white and one black middle-class citizens doesn't think he ought to be punished because people in the black ghetto have their own rules and mores? That Willie Franklin is innocent and should go free? I'm not certain what the Franklin jury will decide, but fortunately, given my restless nature, I won't have to wait long before I find out.

2:37 P.M.

"Betsy, I want to draft my Gilbert opinion this after-noon, so hold all my calls," Barth says. "Except, of course, if the Franklin jury comes in with a verdict." Barth then shuts the door to his chambers and assembles the materials he will need, including last week's Gilbert hearing transcript, the most recent bound volumes of decisions by the State Court of Appeals, and a volume of the *State Code of Criminal Procedure*. He sits down at his conference table and begins to write on a yellow legal pad:

(197)

On the afternoon of February 2, 1973, the defendant, armed with a .32-caliber revolver, and another man forced their way into the safe deposit department of the First National Bank. After the bank officer on duty was bound and gagged, the defendant looted 22 safe deposits boxes of $2.5 million in jewelry and other valuables. Six days later, police arrested the defendant, Roger Gilbert, for the crime, searched his apartment and seized more than $1.4 million in jewelry and other valuables. It was later determined that the loot had been stolen from the First National Bank safe deposit boxes.

Roger Gilbert was brought to trial on June 18, 1973, in the courtroom of Judge Randolph Pearson of the State Criminal Court. On July 20, 1973, Gilbert pleaded guilty in open court to the charge of attempted armed robbery in the first degree. Under the State Penal Code, Section 472, the plea of attempted robbery in the first degree permits a sentence range between zero and fifteen years in prison. No promise of a sentence maximum was entered on the record.

On December 17, 1973, Judge Pearson sentenced the defendant, Roger Gilbert, to fifteen years in the state penitentiary. By this application, under the State Code of Criminal Procedure, Section 342, the petitioner, Roger Gilbert, seeks an order setting aside the judgment of conviction on the ground that his plea of guilty was induced by coercive means, including the promise from the Court that a lesser sentence, not exceeding five years, would be imposed.

The following facts were established at the hearing on the petitioner's motion to set aside the judgment. On June 18, 1973, the first witness was called on the defendant's pre-trial motion to suppress evidence seized by police at the defendant's apartment. After the suppression hearing had begun, but before any ruling on the motion had been made, Judge Pearson ordered jury selection to begin. Both prosecution and defense counsel objected to the beginning of the jury selection, arguing that failure to decide the suppression motion before the selection of the jury was a violation of the State Code of Criminal Procedure, Section 256. Moreover, counsel argued that the Court's decision on the suppression motion would influence counsel's strategy at jury selection and, ultimately, affect the outcome of the trial. (Barnes, *Hearing Minutes,* pp. 42–45; Rollins, *Hearing Minutes,* pp. 165–7). Despite these arguments, Judge Pearson ordered that the jury selection proceed at the same time that he was hearing witnesses for the suppression motion. For the next four weeks, Judge Pearson presided over the suppression hearing in the mornings and the jury selection in the afternoons. Neither was completed.

While presiding over the suppression hearing and jury selection, Judge Pearson also initiated plea-bargaining discussions with counsel. According to testimony from both prosecution and defense attorneys, Judge Pearson discussed both the plea and his anticipated ruling on the suppression hearing at the meetings, hinting of an adverse ruling, first to one side and then to the other, if there was no plea. (Barnes, *Hearing Minutes,* pp. 67–69; Rollins, *Hearing Minutes,* p. 173). In his testimony, Judge Pearson characterized the plea discussions in the following way: "I indicated to them that it looked to me like a very close question and could go either way. Under such circumstances, it would seem to me that sensible people ought to talk about what ought to be done." (Judge Pearson, *Hearing Minutes,* pp. 378, 379). Judge Pearson took counsel to lunch, at which time these discussions continued. *(Hearing Minutes,* p. 245). Judge Pearson later testified that he discussed a five-year sentence with Gilbert and his attorney, but he said that he made no promises (Pearson, *Hearing Minutes,* p. 378).

But on July 19, 1973, according to the testimony of the defendant, Gilbert, and his counsel, Whitney Barnes, Judge Pearson promised, in exchange for a plea of attempted armed robbery, that the defendant would be sentenced to no more than five years in prison. That promise was not entered on the record. Barnes testified: "Judge Pearson told me that he would not sentence my client to more than five years. 'I can give him as little as I want,' Judge Pearson told me, 'but it won't be more than five years.' " (Barnes, *Hearing Minutes,* p. 301). Later, according to both defense counsel's testimony and that of the defendant, Gilbert, Judge Pearson again called them into his chambers and indicated, by both word and gesture, that he would not sentence Gilbert to more than five years. "Judge Pearson held up his hands to us, displaying five fingers. Then he leaned back in his chair and told us to trust him. I'll never forget that scene as long as I live. He propped his feet up on his desk and said, 'Trust me, fellas. I have your best interest at heart. Trust me.' And we trusted him. (Barnes, *Hearing Minutes,* p. 311). The defendant, Gilbert, testified: "Judge Pearson said, 'Trust me.' The judge said he wouldn't give me more than five years. And then he raised five fingers. He said, 'I won't tell you what the sentence will be but it won't be more than five years.' And I asked him if he was going to double-cross me and he said again, 'Trust me, trust me.' And I figured if you can't trust a judge, who can you trust?" (Gilbert, *Hearing Minutes,* p. 329).

The rules governing judicial behavior in plea-bargaining are clear: "A guilty plea may be encouraged, but the judicial function should be limited to determining: that its acceptance is in the public interest and receiving assurance from

(200)

the defendant that he understands the nature of the plea; that the plea is freely and voluntarily made with full knowledge of the constitutional rights the defendant is thereby waiving; that the defendant committed the acts to which he is pleading guilty or is knowingly and intelligently willing to plead guilty, without an express admission of guilt, to avoid the consequences of a conviction, and that no promises by way of inducement have been made to defendant by his lawyer, the district attorney, the Court, or anyone else other than those clearly and fully spread on the record." (*People* v. *Rideau*).

The history of this case fails to meet the test of *Rideau*. Specifically, I find:

That plea negotiations were initiated and went forward with Judge Randolph Pearson as an active participant.

That the commencement of jury selection of June 22 was improper in that the pre-trial motions had not been decided.

That the defendant, Roger Gilbert, had reason to believe on July 19 that the trial court would not render a decision on the pre-trial motion as required by statute.

That the petitioner, Gilbert, was advised by his attorney, Whitney Barnes, that Judge Pearson had made a commitment to induce his plea that his sentence would not exceed five years.

That Whitney Barnes reasonably believed, from the words and gestures of Judge Pearson, that the sentence to be imposed on Gilbert would not exceed five years.

That the defendant, Gilbert, relied on the representations made to him by his attorney and on the expressions and statements personally made to him by Judge Pearson that his sentence would not exceed five years.

That the defendant and his attorney reasonably believed that they might accept Judge Pearson's assurance of a five-year sentence without the plea minutes reflecting such a promise.

That Judge Pearson did not place on the record, at the time the pleas were taken, all the facts within his knowledge relating to the events preceding the taking of the plea.

That James Rollins, the assistant district attorney prosecuting the case for the People, was not aware at the time the plea was taken that a promise of a sentence not to exceed five years had been made to the defendant or his attorney during robing room sessions at which he was not present.

Upon all the facts the petitioner, Roger Gilbert, has sustained the burden of proof. The realities of human nature and common experience compel the conclusion that the petitioner did not freely offer a guilty plea. Rather, the plea was the result of the subtly coercive influence exerted by Judge Pearson. I find that Judge Pearson desired that the case be "pleaded out" and made an explicit promise to induce the plea. The promise that was made was not kept.

The sentence of December 17, 1973, is vacated and the defendant, Gilbert, is to be accorded an election as to whether he wishes to be sentenced to an indeterminate sentence with a maximum of five years, or to have the sentence and judgment of conviction vacated and the plea of not guilty reinstated.

For the first time since he pressed his felt pen to paper, Barth looks up. His eyes settle on one of his favorite books, *Confronting Injustice,* on the second shelf of his bookcase. He walks to the bookshelf, pulls out the book, a collection of articles and speeches by Edmond Cahn, and thumbs through it until he finds a favorite Cahn quotation: "For what gives justice its special savor of nobility? Only the divine wrath that arises in us, girds us, and drives us to action whenever an instance of injustice affronts our sight."

(202)

Should I end my opinion with Cahn's quotation? Barth asks himself. No, that's too easy. If I'm going to say something about this business of judging, I'm going to say it in my words and I'm going to direct those words to the specific problems raised by the Gilbert case. Barth carefully places the book back on the shelf, returns to the conference table and begins to write:

The plea bargain is a necessary evil of our system of criminal justice. Without guilty pleas, our court calendars would be so crowded with trials that the system could not function. Guilty pleas, however, should only be encouraged under strict procedures that insure fundamental fairness to all parties involved. Otherwise, we trade justice for efficiency.

A judge has a particularly sensitive role to play in the plea-bargaining process. His influence over the process is clearly greater than that of other participants, whether defendant, defense counsel, or prosecutor. While participating in plea discussions, the judge also has the power to make rulings that may substantially help or harm the case of both prosecution and defense. Not infrequently these rulings on points of law determine whether a defendant goes to prison or walks out of the courtroom a free man.

When a judge participates in plea bargaining, therefore, he must be particularly careful not to abuse the power of his office. He must not manipulate. He must not cajole. He must not threaten. For if he does any of these things, the judge not only destroys the value of the bargain, but also undermines the integrity of the criminal justice system.

(203)

Barth sees the intercom button light up and begins to straighten his tie, anticipating Betsy's message. He picks up the telephone receiver.

"Judge, the Franklin jury has a verdict."

"Okay, Betsy. Tell George I'll be right up."

Barth walks down the corridor alone. Click-clack. Click-clack. The sound reminds Barth of the old Jack Benny radio show when Jack would walk through miles of imaginary underground tunnels in search of his precious vault.

When Barth enters the courtroom, he is greeted by broad smiles from court officers Sam Mitchell and Alfred Lorenzo. Their fear of a late night is now behind them. But there are no smiles for Barth from the Franklin jurors as they walk past the bench. The earlier jauntiness of the foreman is gone. His eleven companions are equally somber.

Willie Franklin is not chewing gum. Otherwise, his manner has not changed from the nonchalance of the morning session. His attorney, Martin Bowers, picks furiously at a hangnail. He is obviously nervous. Prosecutor Tom Snowden is chatting amiably with the court reporter. He is obviously relaxed.

"Will the foreman of the jury and the defendant please rise?" says Giles. The foreman stands as does Willie Franklin. "Has the jury reached a verdict?" asks Giles.

"Yes, we have," replies the foreman.

"On the first count, burglary in the second degree, how do you find the defendant, Willie Franklin?"

"Not guilty."

"On the second count, petty larceny, how do you find the defendant, Willie Franklin?"

"Not guilty."

"On the third count, rape in the first degree, how do you find the defendant, Willie Franklin?"

"Not guilty."

Martin Bowers gives Willie Franklin a hearty clap on the shoulder and shakes his hand vigorously. The defendant seems discomforted by his attorney's effusiveness. He returns Bowers's wide grin with a dutiful smile. Barth discreetly asks George Giles to find out if there are any "holds" on Franklin in other cases. Giles makes two quick phone calls and reports that there are not.

"Mr. Franklin," Barth says, "you are free to leave."

Willie Franklin stuffs a wad of gum in his mouth and shambles out of the courtroom. Martin Bowers bounces along after his client, full of energy and enthusiasm. Tom Snowden quickly clears the prosecutor's table and leaves the courtroom through a side door. The jurors linger a few minutes, chatting among themselves. Then they, too, depart.

"What happened, Judge?" asks George Giles as they wait for the elevator.

"I think it's fairly obvious," Barth replies curtly. "The jury wasn't satisfied with the testimony of Delores Harper and Charles Mapes. That doesn't mean they thought Willie Franklin was innocent. Just looking at those miserable faces as the verdict was announced, you know goddamn well they had their doubts about Mr. Franklin. But the law says guilty beyond a reasonable doubt and, obviously, these people took the law seriously."

As Barth steps into the elevator, Giles gives him a last quizzical look.

"Don't look at me like that, George. Why didn't Delores Harper's boyfriend show up at her apartment that night? And why didn't Charles Mapes call the police after Delores told him she'd been raped? Think about it."

After the elevator doors close, Barth thinks about his own questions. Nah. This is Mr. Franklin's lucky day. He beat the rap. The jury just didn't believe Delores Harper. But why did this jury act differently from the jury that convicted John Harding of assault and armed robbery on Wednesday? The critical question is why Karen Petersen's story of being assaulted and robbed in a fourteenth-floor cafeteria office was believed and Delores Harper's story of being raped in her Grove Street apartment was not. The only reason I can think of is that the Harding jury figured that what happened to Miss Petersen, a white, in her office could happen to them. It's not the same with Mrs. Harper, a black, coming home at midnight without her boyfriend. The jury apparently couldn't identify with her. Even that single black juror. He surprised me. Maybe he fought for Mrs. Harper. But the jury was out less than four hours. So obviously he couldn't have fought too hard.

Justice was done, Barth tells himself. Twelve solid citizens deliberated and found that the prosecution had not proven that the defendant, Willie Franklin, was guilty beyond a reasonable doubt. Some judges might be upset if they felt, as I do, that Franklin was guilty. I'm not. My responsibility was to see that the evidence was presented fairly. I did that. The jury's responsibility was to evaluate the evidence presented at the trial in a fair and impartial way. They did that and concluded that the prosecution had not removed all serious doubts about the question of Willie Franklin's guilt.

So now there is one more rapist loose in this city, Barth mutters. Willie Franklin will probably be back. In fact, I'm sure of that.

Barth wants something, anything to take his mind off Willie Franklin and Jesse Norwood and Robert Lindsay and the whole miserable judicial day. His thoughts turn to the opera tonight. *Don Giovanni.* At least there I'll be assured of dramatic certainty as well as artistic perfection. I know, goddamnit, that Don Giovanni will kill the Commendatore in the first act and go to hell in the last. It has been that way for more than 175 years and there'll be no change tonight.

The thought pleases him. He walks down the corridor
singing:

> *Questo è il fin*
> *di chi fa mal*
> *E dé perfidi la morte*
> *alla vita è sempre ugual.**

---

* TRANSLATION: "Such is the end of those who do evil. The death of the wicked always
matches their life."

About the Author

James F. Simon received a B.A. from Yale College and a law degree from the Yale Law School. He has served as correspondent and contributing editor of *Time* magazine, specializing in legal affairs. His first book, *In His Own Image: The Supreme Court in Richard Nixon's America,* won the American Bar Association's Silver Gavel Award in 1974. He has been a Visiting Lecturer in American Studies at Yale University and a Harvard Fellow in Law and the Humanities at Harvard University. He currently teaches law at New York Law School and the City College of New York, and lives with his wife and two children in West Nyack, New York. He comes from a Texas family with a long, distinguished legal tradition.